HEMINGWAY

AN OLD FRIEND REMEMBERS

Jed Kiley

HAWTHORN BOOKS, INC.
Publishers   New York City

First Edition, April, 1965

PUBLISHER'S
INTRODUCTION

"You can write anything you please as you recollect it about me," wrote Ernest Hemingway from his Finca Vigia in Cuba to Jed Kiley at the Overseas Press Club in New York in the Fall of 1954. "But," Hemingway continued, "please don't expect me to authenticate it or authorize it."

"Good luck with everything you write," the same letter went on.

But Jed Kiley's luck was not very good. Although he sold his series of articles on his recollections of Hemingway to *Playboy*, where they appeared during 1956 and 1957, he wrote little thereafter. He died in New York in 1962 at the age of 73, a year after his old friend's tragic death.

In the Twenties, Floyd Gibbons, the most famous correspondent of his day, called him "the best known American in Paris" and the Sunday magazine supplements ran full-page features about the visits of the then Prince of Wales to "Kiley's," his Montmartre night club. A guide book of the day listed Kiley as one of the five Americans who had left the greatest mark on Paris.

John Gerald Kiley was born in Chicago, Illinois, on June 10, 1889. Educated at St. Viator's in Bourbonnais, Illinois, and the University of Wisconsin, he became a reporter on the Chicago *Examiner*. In later years, he was remembered there for, among other things, being the first Chicago reporter ever to own an automobile. His association with that newspaper ceased when, sent to cover the departure of the First Illinois Cavalry for the Mexican border, he and Charles MacArthur, then of the Chicago *Examiner*, enlisted in a flush of patriotism. His editor, the famous Walter Howey, later immortalized by MacArthur in *The Front Page*, when told by Kiley of this change in status, is reported to have answered, "Listen, no one gets to be a hero on this paper unless I order it."

The adventures of Kiley and MacArthur in Mexico are still the subject of gossip when newspapermen of their generation talk about old times. Eventually, Kiley was mustered out of the National Guard and, after a brief stint on the Chicago *Tribune*, by 1917 was in Paris as a driver for the American Field Service. During this period, he became very friendly with Floyd Gibbons, who was the *Tribune*'s war correspondent. When the United States entered the war, Kiley joined the American army in

6

the Service of Supply and remained in Paris. He obtained his discharge from the army there and took his first steps toward becoming a night club entrepreneur by organizing a series of dances for officers. Dancing was forbidden in Paris at that time, as an austerity measure in the immediate postwar period, but Kiley managed to promote enough dances to acquire sufficient capital to purchase the Y.M.C.A.'s ice cream manufacturing machinery when that organization closed down its wartime operation.

Kiley's ice cream business, although initially successful, was short-lived; he had not reckoned on the reluctance of Europeans to buy ice cream in the wintertime. This was followed by a series of other enterprises, including the opening of a restaurant and night club called "Kiley's," in the Rue Fontaine in Montmartre.

The new cabaret was a success. Kiley introduced some of the first Negro jazz bands and blues singers to Paris and attracted such distinguished patrons as the Prince of Wales. Both his attractions and his patrons followed him to another Montmartre night club, the "College Inn," which he opened on the Rue Vavin.

One of his patrons and good friends was a rich young man named Erskine Gwynne, a great-grandson of *the* Mrs. Cornelius Vanderbilt. In 1927, Gwynne started a magazine in Paris called *The Boulevardier*, somewhat similar in approach to *The New Yorker*. It was edited by Arthur Moss, and Kiley became assistant editor. This was Kiley's second journalistic fling in Paris; his first was a few months on the Paris *Herald* in 1918 which Eric Hawkins later referred to in his *Hawkins of the Paris Herald* as a "brief moment in the newspaper business as a springboard to bigger and better things." During Kiley's tenure with *The Boulevardier,* its contributors included Hemingway, F. Scott Fitzgerald, Louis Bromfield, Sinclair Lewis, Noel Coward and Rube Goldberg, among others.

A mutual interest in prize fighting had brought Hemingway and Kiley together for the first time in Chicago before World War I. The war later took both of them to Paris, but their interests drifted apart. Their renewed friendship was even more surprising because Hemingway's Paris was the Paris of the Left Bank and Montparnasse while Kiley's was the Paris of the Right Bank and Montmartre. But Kiley, in his capacity as "the best known American in Paris" made friends with a wide variety of people, and Floyd Gibbons was able to quote some of them on the subject of Kiley. Sinclair Lewis called him "a sheep in wolf's clothing." O. O. McIntyre, the columnist, said he was "a poet in the guise of an inn keeper." And Frazier Hunt referred to him simply as "that amazing American."

The Boulevardier died of financial anemia in 1931, but Kiley had already returned to the United States at the end of 1929, to work as a screen writer for Carl Laemmle, Jr., at Universal Pictures. His

8

departure coincided with the aftermath of the stock market crash and the beginning of the Great Depression, which marked the end of the glittering and glamorous Paris Kiley and his friends had known. When Hemingway returned, his haunt became the Ritz bar rather than a table on the terrace of the Rotonde or the Sélect; when Kiley returned, the old buildings were gone along with the old cronies and only the old memories were left.

Kiley spent some four years in Hollywood after leaving Paris, working as a screen writer and later operating an athletic center at Santa Monica. From there, he moved to Miami, Florida, where he renewed his friendship with Floyd Gibbons, by then a leading radio commentator. In Gibbons' company, Kiley visited Key West and Cuba a number of times and made at least one visit of several weeks' duration to Hemingway's home near Havana.

In 1939, Kiley helped promote the World's Fair in New York City. From 1943 to 1946, he published a series of articles on such varied subjects as confidence men, Monte Carlo, Al Capone, and the Gestapo in *True Detective* magazine. He traveled, revisiting Paris at the age of 70, and, shortly before his death, he made a trip to Japan and the Philippines. On his return, he visited an old friend of his Paris days, Basil Woon, in Carson City, Nevada, and then went on to Las Vegas, where his weakening condition resulted in his hospitalization. After his release from the hospital, he went to Chicago to visit his sister, Eileen, and then on to New York, where he died shortly afterward.

Kiley's work on Hemingway was called to this publisher's attention by a letter from a friend of Kiley, John Guenther, of Rye, New York, which appeared in the *Times Literary Supplement* of London on July 9, 1964, calling the original *Playboy* articles "one of the best portraits of the real Hemingway now available to us." By this time, both the author and his subject were dead. Finding the original manuscript, locating the author's heirs and gathering the information which appears here about Kiley's own life, the Paris of his time and his relationship with Ernest Hemingway has indebted the publisher to many people, in the United States and abroad, to whom grateful acknowledgment is made. They include Harry Arnold, Joseph A. Barry, Eileen M. Cooney, Donna Hamilton Fifield, Florence Gilliam, John Guenther, Minna Harkavy, Eric Hawkins, Wolfe Kaufman, Frances Jones, Harold Loeb, Janine Spanier Metz, Arthur Moss, Frank Jerome Riley, A. C. Spectorsky, Virgil Thomson, Alice B. Toklas, H.R.H. the Duke of Windsor, and Basil Woon. Mr. Barry and Mr. Woon, in particular, supplied most of the information upon which this introductory note has been based.

PREFACE*

THIS round-by-round account of a one-sided prize fight was written by the loser, years before the tragic death of the Winner-and-Still-Champion, Ernest Miller Hemingway. It was written shortly after he had won the title in Stockholm in 1954.

Should the gore in some of the rounds displease you, turn away as some of us do at bullfights, but never forget that it was written as a tribute to a great man.

If you think it irreverent—that's fine. Papa was the most irreverent person I ever knew, both in his writings and in his conversation. If you think there is too much drinking of hard liquor in it, then you just did not know the Champ.

Ernest was the world's most controversial

* The author died in 1962 having written no introduction for this book. The publisher has created this preface from passages in various letters and other writings of the author.

writer, and his death came the same way his stories ended—with the reader still guessing. His "mysterious" death received more publicity than that of any other celebrity in history. F.D.R.'s death during a world war did not get one tenth of the words written about it as Hemingway's.

Even at the end, he was the publicity man of the age. Barnum had nothing on Papa. Since his death the millions of words pounded out by his admirers make him another god and never mention the idol's feet of clay. Those biographers who have were too bitter.

Ernest did everything the hard way. He worked hard, played hard, drank hard, fought hard, and even died the hard way. I think he would have liked this verse by the late Edna St. Vincent Millay for his epitaph:

> My candle burns at both the ends;
>   It will not last the night;
> But ah, my foes and oh, my friends—
>   It gives a lovely light.

CONTENTS

ILLUSTRATIONS

HEMINGWAY
AN OLD FRIEND REMEMBERS

The Sun Also Rises

He was standing next to me at the bar. He was a big fellow. About twenty-five, I thought. He needed a shave and a haircut. And his sport coat looked like he had slept in it. But you could see he was not a barfly. He threw out a big hand in my direction. It was a hand you would not want thrown at you in anger. His coat sleeves were short and you could see the heavy, black hair on his thick wrists. He had a short, black mustache that looked like his eyebrows. He grinned all over. It was a pleasant grin, I thought. I winced as we shook hands. Some grip.

"Hello," he said.

"Hello," I said.

"Remember me?" he said.

"Sure, sure," I said.

Who is this guy? I thought. Must have

met him up at my place in Montmartre. I had an American night club up on the Hill and everybody knew me. You could see he was a Yank by the way he held his drink. Had a death-grip on it. Like somebody was going to take it away from him. But that did not mean a thing. They had Prohibition then back in the States and that's the way all the tourists drank. Like somebody was going to take it away from them. Some law, I thought.

I said aloud, "Have a drink?"

"Why not?" he said.

He knocked off his old drink at a gulp. You could not see what he was drinking. His big hand hid the glass. Alphonse brought us two *fines*. He had a paw wrapped around his before it hit the bar. Some hands. Wonder what he does, I thought. Probably one of those sculptors from the Left Bank. Did not seem to be holding enough dough for a tourist. Must have met him in one of the bars. Some drinker. Better let him talk some more.

"Been reading your stuff in *The Boulevardier*," he said.

Well, I thought, that's different. Erskine Gwynne and I were getting out a smart little magazine on the Champs Elysées and I was the top writer. They used to read my stuff in *The*

20

Boulevardier and then came up the Hill to meet the author. You might say I was literary in the daytime and mercenary at night. I liked to talk about my stuff too. So I hooked my cane over the bar rail and ordered a refill on the *fines*. If there's one thing an author likes it's honest criticism from a stranger.

"Like it?" I said.

"No," he said.

"Oh," I said. "What are you doing here besides drinking?"

"Writing," he said.

"Writing what?" I said.

"A book," he said.

"Oh," I said.

This bird is a wise guy, I thought. He has probably been around Paris all of three weeks, and he is writing a book about it. That is the way a lot of them did. They sat around the Dôme drinking *fines* and Pernods and wrote books about Paris. Then you never heard about them again. I had been around Paris for six years and still did not know enough about Paris to write a book about it. Maybe that's the way it was. The longer you stayed around the less you wanted to write a book about it.

"Like it over here?" I said.

"No," he said.

21

Better get out of here fast, I thought. The man's a poseur. Who ever heard of an American not liking Paris? No wonder he didn't like my stuff. The guy's taste is all in his mouth. I hooked the Malacca back on my arm and gave him the old night-club smile.

"Nice seeing you again, Doc," I said.

He roared out laughing and slapped me on the back. I can still feel it.

"The name's Hemingway," he said.

Well, what do you know, I thought. It's old Ernest Miller Hemingway from Oak Park. Nobody else could have a name like that. Had not seen him since the war. Knew he was in Europe somewhere. He had come over in the French Ambulance in '17 when I had. But he had been in an Italian section. Heard he had enlisted in the Italian army and had been badly wounded. I hung the cane back on the bar and shook hands again. There's nothing wrong with his grip, I thought.

"Didn't know you with the false mustache," I said.

"Bar stance is changed too," he said.

That's right, I thought. Used to stand with the other leg on the rail. No wonder I didn't recognize him. Must be that war wound, I thought.

I said aloud, "Have a drink."

"Sure," he said louder.

Hasn't changed a bit, I thought. He was quite an amateur boxer, I remembered. Used to say he was going to be the world's heavyweight champion some day. And he might have made it. Guess the wound must have knocked that idea out of his head, I thought.

"Still going to be the Champ?" I said.

"Yes," he said, "but not in boxing."

"Wrestling?" I said.

"No," he said.

"What?" I said.

"Literature," he said.

"Oh," I said.

Still shooting at the moon, I thought. Never pulls his punches. Always in there trying. Why, when he was a kid in school he used to pick up a tough five bucks acting as a sparring partner for the pros in O'Connell's gym. He didn't care how big they were either. Plenty of guts. Well, he could count on me to be in his corner over here. I knew the ropes. You know how it is when you run into a guy from your own home town. Might start by running something for him in *The Boulevardier*. You could see he could use the prestige. If he can write like he can drink, I thought, I'll take him in my stable.

I said aloud, "What's your record?"

"Just a couple of amateur warm-ups," he said. "Three stories and ten poems and a six-rounder called *In Our Time*."

"Kayos?" I said.

"No," he said. "Didn't want to hurt my hands. I'm turning pro in my next bout. It's an eight-rounder that will put me in the semifinals. Then when I get into the main bouts and grab those big purses in the States I'm going to buy me a boat, a house on a tropical island, and go fishing."

"And retire with the title?" I said.

"No," he said, "I'll defend the title. You know, fight in spurts. Stall for the first two minutes of each round and then go in slugging the last minute like the champs do."

He's got it all figured out, I thought. Sounds like he means it too.

"What's this eight-rounder you're writing?" I said.

"*The Sun Also Rises*," he said.

"Come again," I said.

"*The Sun Also Rises*," he said.

The sun also rises, I thought. What the hell has the sun got to do with Paris? You never see it. You go to bed when it rises and you get up when it sets. What a title for a book on Paris, I thought.

24

"Better call it the moon also rises," I said aloud.

"Gertrude likes it," he said.

"Gertrude who?" I said.

"Gertrude Stein," he said. "She's my trainer."

Holy smokes, I thought. A chump is a chump is a chump. If he listens to those Left Bank oracles he's going to be throwing iambic tetrameters instead of punches. Better get him across the river and under the trees of the Champs Elysées fast.

"Ernest," I said, "how would you like to do a one-round benefit for *The Boulevardier?* If you got something short and sweet with a wallop I can run it for you. No purse, as you know, but plenty of prestige."

"Glad to help you boys out," he said.

"Well, it would help you, too," I said. "To have the name Ernest Miller Hemingway up there with Sinclair Lewis, Scott Fitzgerald, and the rest of us."

"I have dropped the Miller," he said.

"OK," I said, "I'll call you Kid Hemingway if you like. What kind of stuff are you doing?"

He feinted with his left, shot a straight right and picked up a big envelope from the bar.

"Here's a short left hook," he said. "Travels only about eight inches but carries authority. If it isn't a knockout, I'll eat it. It's not for *The Boulevardier*, however. You guys would duck and let it go over your heads."

Oh yeah, I thought. I opened it up and looked at the title. "The Killers" it was called. I'll say it's not for us, I thought. "The Kissers" would have pleased me better. I ordered another round to give me strength, and glanced through the manuscript.

The story was all dialogue. It was all right as far as it went but it didn't get anywhere. Some gangsters were going to kill a Swede. They walked into a cafe where the Swede used to eat and waited for him with their hands in their pockets. Then they walked out. The Swede came in later and when he heard they had been looking for him he couldn't eat. Just went home to his furnished room and went to bed. That's the way it ended. With the poor Swede waiting in bed. Sort of left you up in the air.

"Where's the rest of it?" I said.

"The rest of what?" he said.

"The story," I said.

"Don't be silly," he said, "that's my style."

Well, if that's his style I'll take vanilla, I thought.

"I'm sending it that way to the States," he asserted.

"Listen, kid," I said, "you gotta have a Hollywood ending for the States. Take a tip from me and have the two killers give it to the Swede with Tommy guns. They step out of the clothes closet and give it to him while he is saying his prayers. Then you got something."

"I'll make a note of that," he said.

I didn't like the way he said it. But I'll bet he does change it, I thought. If he doesn't they'll blast him.

Then he shadow boxed, drove a hard right into the inside pocket of his sports coat and hit me with a few crumpled sheets of yellow paper written in lead pencil.

"Here's a low kidney punch for that throw-away of yours," he said. "Don't change a word."

Get a load of that, I thought. Don't change a word. Here I am doing the guy a favor, and he starts ordering me around. I tell him how to end the killers thing and he fouls me. Offer to print his stuff in *The Boulevardier* and he calls it a "throwaway." What if he does know the magazine, I thought. He doesn't know me well enough to call it that to my face.

I glanced at the title. It was "The Real Spaniard." Sounded all right. Louis Bromfield,

27

another young Paris writer, had done a piece for us called "The Real French." Louis had already hit the jackpot with his second book. It got him the Pulitzer Prize. That meant the other Left Bank writers would be out gunning for him, I thought.

"Parody on Bromfield?" I said.

"Yeah," he said. "I give him hell."

That's OK, I thought. We liked parodies in the book. But I didn't say anything. Just stuck the thing in my pocket without reading it. Might need it for wrapping up a parcel some day. I was still sore about that crack he had made about the magazine. Better change the subject, I thought. One more drink and I'd be telling him what he could do with his wrapping paper. I put on my phony night-club smile.

I said, "Ever been up to my place on the Hill?"

"No," he said.

"Why?" I said.

"Too high," he said.

"The Hill?" I said.

"No. The prices," he said.

I said, "Come up any night. Be my guest. Bring your girl."

"Thanks," he said.

"Got a *smoking?*" I said.

"A what?" he said.

"A *smoking*," I said.

Can you beat that, I thought. He is writing a book on Paris and he does not know what a *smoking* is. A *smoking* is Paris argot for a tuxedo, I told him. You got to be dressed in my place. It's no Left Bank honky-tonk. We open at midnight and close when the sun also rises, I told him. Might as well impress him that it was a classy joint. He might think it is another Hinkey Dinks in Chicago, I thought.

"There's no sawdust on my floor," I said.

"Too bad," he said. "But I will give you a break for old time's sake. I never play when I work but I will come up when the book is finished. I'll bring Lady Brett with me."

"Lady who?" I said.

"Lady Brett," he said. "Belongs to an old English family, title and all that sort of thing. You wouldn't know her."

"Oh," I said.

"I'll bring you an autographed copy of the book too," he said.

"Thanks," I said. And I paid the check and left the bar.

I had to laugh when I got outside. Here I had a whole bookcase full of autographed best sellers like Sinclair Lewis' *Main Street*, Michael

Arlen's *The Green Hat,* Scott Fitzgerald's *The Great Gatsby,* and a lot of others. And that kid was going to give me an autographed copy of his opus. Not only that, he was going to lend a little class to my place by bringing Lady What's-Her-Name. Why, ever since the Prince of Wales started coming there I had them all. Wait until he sees the cream of British nobility hobnobbing with me, I thought. Lady Mountbatten used to say my dance floor looked like an illustrated copy of Burke's Peerage. The Duke of Manchester was there every night. They liked my jazz band The Crackerjacks and the Argentine orchestra specializing in the tango, which was a new wrinkle then. Well, I thought, I only hope his story is up to *The Boulevardier's* standards. Those standards were high in one way and low in another. Look at Sinclair Lewis. He made the Nobel Prize, but he had a tough time making *The Boulevardier.* We turned him down twice. His stuff was too provincial for us.

In the taxi to the office I got thinking about Lewis. The only way he resembles Hemingway, I thought, is in his drinking. He was a swell guy though. He finally did make the magazine, too. That was when I cut a five thousand-word yarn of his down to one thousand. He was delighted to make the grade and bought up half

30

the issue to send to friends in the States. Never could do the short stuff, he always said. Nice guy. You don't mind helping out a writer like that, I thought.

I showed "The Real Spaniard" to Gwynne and told him Hemingway was another Bromfield. Gwynne read it, hit the ceiling, and grabbed a big blue pencil. "Where does he write, on restroom walls?" he roared. I looked over his shoulder and there were two four-letter words. They were words that you heard around the office all the time. But you didn't see them.

"Well," I said, "he spelled them correctly didn't he?"

And the guy tells me not to change a word, I thought. Gwynne tossed the sheets over to Arthur Moss. Arthur was the editor and said he knew Hemingway and wasn't surprised. He read the piece through and then turned over the last page. "Where's the rest of it?" he said. "You must have lost a page."

"That's all he gave me," I said. I read it myself. It's an unfinished symphony, I thought. But maybe he wants it like that.

I said aloud, "It's the latest style in literature and—" I added, "he comes from my home town."

31

"OK," Moss said. "Write an ending to it and we'll run it on page forty-two."

"Not me," I said. "Promised I wouldn't change a word."

"You don't have to change a word," Arthur said. "Just add a paragraph. I'll take the rap for you if he squawks. We go to press in an hour and we can't print it that way. The story stinks and you know it."

Of course I knew it. But I knew Hemingway too. Well, I thought, if he didn't give me all of it it's not my fault. Besides, Moss had agreed to take the blame. I wanted the yarn to get in that issue, and it wouldn't make the grade the way it was.

So I wrote an ending. I ghosted his style a little and it turned out swell. The story wasn't bad at all with my ending. Then we ran a little blurb about his book. That ought to please him, I thought.

But it didn't please him. The magazine was hardly on the stands before he was on our necks. Came roaring into the office with fire in his eye and said I had spoiled the story. I told the truth; said I had not changed a word. I should have stood in bed like the guy in the other story, I thought. I glanced over at Moss. Would he take the rap as he had promised?

Li'l Abner, as we called him, stood under five feet and weighed in ringside at 123 pounds. But there was no moss attached to him except his name. He had to bend his head away back to look at our detractor, but he looked the bull right in the eye.

"Pipe down, big boy," he said. "I'm the editor and I rewrote your story for the better. What are you going to do about it?" Ernest looked like he couldn't believe his ears. He bent over to get a better look.

"Stand up and I'll show you," he said.

"I am standing up," Arthur said, and he really was.

That broke the spell. Ernest stuck out a big hand. I knew he would.

"Shake, brother," he said. "You got guts."

Then he walked out without a glance at me. That's gratitude for you, I thought. You try to help out a pal and he does not appreciate it. Show him how to write and he says you spoiled his story. Well, let him go back to his Gertrude Stein and see if I care. Bet that book of his needs a rewrite more than the story did, I thought.

I didn't see my new fighter for a couple of months. Heard he was holed up working on the proofs of that opus of his. Then he dropped into

33

my place one night, and the minute I saw what he had with him I was sure he was still sore at me for that rewrite job. She was awful. Of all the females in the entire world there was only one barred permanently from my place. And he had her on his arm. How she ever got by Blink Mc-Clusky at the door I'll never know. Must have come up on his blind side. How she ever got across the river was a mystery. Like Chicago's West Side hoboes, who were barred from crossing the Chicago River, she was barred socially from the Montmartre night spots across the Seine. Her natural habitat was the Left Bank. Some gal.

I didn't object to her on moral grounds. My place was no church. It was the way she behaved and the way she dressed. They say she was from a good family in England but they paid her a small remittance to stay out of the British Isles. If she crossed the Channel the dough stopped. She was a table-hopper and generally wore soiled tennis shoes and a pair of men's pants. That was long before they called them "slacks" and normal women took to wearing them.

And here she was with Hemingway. Had used him to crash the gate. Well, I had asked for it. The waiters were ganging up for the bum's rush but I waved them aside. He looked pretty good. Almost civilized. Had a *smoking* on and

was even shaved. Maybe he just looks good alongside of her, I thought. As I came up you could
see he was ready to present me as they do at the
Court of St. James's. But she put her hand up in
the air as though she were reaching for a strap in
a bus, to shake hands.

"Fawncy seeing you here," she said.

"Fancy seeing *you* here," I said.

"Fancy your knowing Lady Brett," he
responded.

Lady Brett! I thought. Is this the one he
calls Lady Brett? That was a new moniker to me.
I had heard her called many things but never
that. They called her "The Countess" around the
Dôme.

I gave the headwaiter the high sign, and
he showed Ernest to a nice table in the back row
behind the post. She hooked her arm in mine.
That gave me a chance to talk to her man to man.
I told her to keep off the dance floor and not
bother any of the guests and she could stay this
time.

Of course I didn't dare to sit down with
them. Had my social position to consider. The
other girls might think she was going to work in
the place and I didn't want any labor trouble
that night. So I said I was very busy and tipped
off Blink to keep an eye on her but not to get into

35

an argument with Hemingway. Blink had lost an eye fighting Jack Johnson and I didn't want him to lose the other one.

She surprised me by behaving herself. Once I heard a scream and a crash from their side of the room and went tearing over there. But it was only one of our regular society matrons slugging it out with a gigolo.

My guests left about five o'clock and left five empty champagne bottles behind them. That's the way we kept count: by leaving the empties on the table. I didn't mind that. But I was a little sore at him for bringing that broad into the place. I went to the *vestiaire* with them. Nobody could see us there. Then he pulled out his book. I'd forgotten all about it. But I had not forgotten the title when I saw it: *The Sun Also Rises*. So I let him have it.

"Where do you think you are?" I said. "In Atlantic City? You don't see any sun around this town, do you? That high flush you are wearing is not sunburn. It's a barroom tan. You should have named it something else when I told you before."

Guess he thought I was kidding because he didn't get mad. Just grinned and wrote something on the flyleaf and handed it to me. I read it. "What's in a name?" it said. "A rose by any

36

other name would smell as sweet." Just some more of the Gertrude Stein stuff, I thought. I flicked over the pages to show a little interest and two words jumped right out and hit me in the eye. "Lady Brett!" I said aloud.

"Yes," he said. "That's the name I gave the Countess in the book. She is my heroine."

"Your heroine of what?" I said.

"Of *The Sun Also Rises*," he said.

"Oh," I said.

"Had a fine time," he said.

"We're even," I said.

"*Au revoir,*" she said.

"Goodbye," I said.

Good Lord, I thought. How do they get that naïve? Some heroine. Well, that's one book I'll never read. And he will never be able to go back to Oak Park after this. They will even give him the horse laugh in Paris. Maybe he was just kidding me, I thought. I opened the book again and glanced through it. There she was all right. Big as life. That bout is not a semifinal, I thought. It's a final with a capital *F*.

But there was something nice about him just the same. Take the time at the Vélodrome d'Hiver. It happened at one of their weekly fights. I was sitting in the front row of the ring-side seats with two lovely American girls when a pug I had had some trouble with walked up to me. I should have recognized his cauliflower ears but I didn't. It was between bouts and he must have been acting as a second since he had a wet sponge in his hand. I put out my hand absently to shake hands with him and he put out his. But he didn't shake hands; instead he shoved the wet sponge in my face and began insulting me.

The crowd loved it. It was a Charlot comedy to them. I was the gent in the *smoking* getting the custard pie from the guy in the sweater. I jumped up to grap the sponge. But as I did two other guys grabbed me. It was three to one. Well, a lot of people in those ringside seats knew me but who do you suppose was the only one to take my part? Right. Monsieur Hemingway. He appeared from nowhere. He was grinning from ear to ear. But he wasn't fooling. He grabbed the two pugs, each by an arm, and pulled the two of them from me as though they were babies. "Get the sponge," he said. "I'll take care of these two punks."

That was all the moral and physical support I needed. I snatched the sponge from the Ears and went into a clinch. Couldn't touch him. Two gendarmes, acting like referees, broke us apart and led us to our corners. But I took a chance and let the sponge go. It was a lucky shot. Just missed the other gendarme and caught the Ears smack in the face. The crowd roared its approval. The gendarmes laughed and I took a bow to the gallery. But when I returned to raise Hemingway's hand he was gone. He had disappeared as mysteriously as he had appeared.

What a strange mixture of guts and diffidence, I thought. He had not hesitated to take a hand in a friend's quarrel in front of the whole crowd. Might even have caused a riot if somebody had started swinging. Then the minute the danger is over he fades out of the picture. Funny guy, all right. They say that when the Italians decorated him they had to bring the medal to him. Afraid to get up in front of the outfit. Not afraid of action but afraid of praise. The girls said he limped a little. Who wouldn't, I thought, with an artificial kneecap and a hundred shell splinters in his body. But that didn't stop him. Some character.

I sure felt grateful to him that night. Kept thinking about it all during the fights. And you could see that the pug who started it was thinking about it too. Kept glaring at me. He was no practical joker either. We had had some serious trouble, and he had threatened to get me.

When the fights were over I began to get worried. Sure wished my bodyguard had stuck

39

around. I told the girls if anything started they were to keep right on going and meet me at the car. As we got into the crush headed for the exit I had a feeling we were being followed. So I dropped back a little and glanced over my shoulder. And sure enough the big guy was right behind me. He was still grinning.

"Keep going," he said. "I'm doing a rear-guard action."

What do you know, I thought. Some friend. He may not be much of a writer but he sure has hair on his chest. He tailed me and I tailed the girls right into my car and in a few minutes we were on our way. I introduced him to the girls. And then they burned me up.

"You're not the Mr. Hemingway who wrote *The Sun Also Rises*, are you?" they both said at once.

"Guilty," he said.

"We both read it and think it's wonderful," they said. And they went on gushing like a couple of bobby-soxers. I didn't mind too much about the brunette. She was a spare. But the redhead was putting it on too thick to suit me. She was sitting up front with me but kept turning around to talk to him. I was glad when he shut her off. He poked his finger in my back.

"How did you like the book?" he said.

Well, I thought, if he thinks I am going to flatter him, just because he saved my life, he's got another think coming. Better give it to him straight from the shoulder.

"I couldn't read the thing," I said.

"Wait a minute," he said.

"Yes," I said.

"Do you move your lips when you read?" he said.

"No," I said.

"That's it," he said.

"That's what," I said.

"That's it. I write for people who move their lips when they read."

"Oh," I said.

The girls laughed their heads off. But I didn't laugh. Bad taste, I thought. I wanted him to ask me why I couldn't read his book. Had some sound criticisms all ready for him. And he laughs it off. Not only that; I had to sit there and listen to the girls raving about it. They wanted to know all about Lady Brett. What a character. Did she really exist? They should ask me, I thought. I could have told them plenty.

I listened to their flattery and got a line on the kind of book it was. Some guy had been fouled in the war. Hit below the belt. He had been Lady Brett's heavy lover before he got the

TKO and when he came out she loved him just the same and continued to live with him. She was even keeping him, according to the story. Baloney, I thought. All that baby ever kept was the change when somebody gave her over two dollars. She was no more capable of spiritual love than I was. Then I heard the story switched to bullfighting in Spain. Bull-throwing is more like it, I thought.

I was burning at this snake I had taken into the bosom of my car. I recall leaning over and whispering into the ear of the redhead that Hemingway himself was the guy who had been shot in the book. I don't recall mentioning that he had been shot in the knee either. All's fair in love and war, I thought.

To Have
and Have Not

It was getting around midnight so I suggested that we all drive up to my place and have a little champagne.

"Sorry," he said. "Told you I never play when I am working. Doing a new book and got to get some sleep."

"OK," I said. "I'll drive you home. Where do you live?"

"Montparnasse," he said.

The redhead said, "What's the book about?"

"Collection of short stories," he said.

I shot over the bridge to the Left Bank and turned up the Boulevard Raspail. So it's short bouts now, I thought. Wonder if he is using that lemon I had read in the bar. "The Killers" or something. Hope the others are better than that one, I thought.

I said aloud. "What kind of stories?"

"I never talk about a story until it is finished," he said. "If you tell it you never write it. The trouble with you is that you tell your stories up at that joint of yours and never write them."

"Oh yeah," I said.

"Yes," he said. "Make up your mind whether you want to be a writer or a saloon-keeper. If you want to run a saloon, keep talking. If you want to be a writer start slugging the typewriter."

"Listen," I said.

"What for?" he said. "I'm not paying you to talk. Put it on paper."

Get a load of that, I thought. You'd think he was Scott Fitzgerald or someone. Here everybody in Paris is talking about my stuff in *The Boulevardier* and he is telling me how to write. What a laugh. Not only that, he probably hasn't got a pot to cook in but he's telling me off right in my own Cadillac. Some gall. Drinks my champagne and calls my joint a saloon. I started to tell him I was a star reporter in Chicago when he was a cub in Kansas City. But the girls were so busy laughing and talking to him I couldn't get a word in edgewise. That's what you get, I thought.

"What's the name of your new book, Mr. Hemingway?" the girls said.

"*Men Without Women*," he said.

"What?" I said.

"*Men Without Women*," he said.

Here's my chance, I thought. Imagine writing a book in Paris with a title like that. First it's *The Sun Also Rises* and now it's *Men Without Women*. Gertrude Stein must have picked that one for him, too, I thought.

I said aloud. "Listen Ernest, let's be Frank and Ernest with each other. Did you ever see a man without a woman in Paris? You are in Paris, France, now, kid, not Paris, Illinois. There are no men without women here and no women without men outside of Lady Brett perhaps."

"Turn left at the cemetery," he said.

"OK," I said. "And while we are here take a good look at that cemetery. If you see any men without women even in there I'll buy you a good dinner. They bury them side by side over there. Hot or cold, in Paris men are with women."

"Third house from the corner," he said.

I stopped at the third house. It was an old brick relic of the Second Empire. It had a

45

Chambres à louer sign in the window and was right across the street from the cemetery. There were no lights on inside but you could see it in spurts. There was a big electric sign on the house next door that flashed on and off. It said *Pompes Funèbres.* Clever idea for an undertaker, I thought. The lights going on and off reminded you that you are here today and gone tomorrow. The house on the other side had a marble orchard in the front yard. It was a monument maker's atelier. The stone angels and other tombstones jumped at you when the undertaker's sign lit up. Nice cheerful spot, I thought. He hopped out like he was going in to the Louvre palace.

"My room's on the fifth floor, girls," he said. "Come up and see me some time."

"Rest in peace," I said.

No wonder he writes that stuff about people getting killed, I thought. He's looking at graves all day. But do you know something? You had to give the guy credit for one thing. He was always himself. Natural like. Look at the way he let me drive him right up to that dump of his. A lot of fellows would have gotten off at the Ritz and walked the rest of the way. But he didn't care. Maybe it's integrity or self-confidence or something. Guess it must be confidence. A Hearst man told me that he had climbed those

46

five flights of stairs around that time to offer him
a newspaper job. The job paid two hundred a
week and he wasn't eating regularly then. But
he turned down the job flat. Said nobody was
going to tell him what to write again. Wanted to
live his own stories. Must have something, I
guess, but you can't put your finger on it.

There's one thing I will say for him though.
He really worked hard. I went around to the
cemetery room one day to see him. The concierge
told me he was there. So I climbed the five flights
and rapped on his door but he wouldn't let me
in. The undertaker's assistant who had the room
next to him told me he had been locked in his
room for a week correcting proofs. Wouldn't let
anybody in. They used to leave coffee and crois-
sants at the door for him. The only exercise he
got was walking to the bathroom at the other
end of the hall. If genius is really the capacity
for taking infinite pains, he *is* a genius, I thought.

But work or no work you could always
see him at the fights. Guess he didn't think going
to the fights was playing; just part of his training.
I used to see him there all the time. We used to
bet ten francs a corner and he almost always
won. We never talked about his books any more.
What's the use, I thought. You can't tell him anything and he won't tell you anything anyway. I

47

didn't mind when he won. Guess he can use the money more than I can, I thought.

When he was not at the fights you knew he was away somewhere. But you never knew where he was. He might be in the green hills of Africa, the blood-soaked arenas of Spain, or somewhere in Italy. He never writes or even sends postals.

It must have been a couple of years before I saw him again.

In November of 1929 the big Depression bounced off of Wall Street and hit Paris hard. It was a TKO for the American colony. Every Yank who had been spending money like water suddenly went dry. They had it one day and didn't have it the next. Forty thousand of them who had been living on incomes fought to get reservations on the boats and borrowed money to pay their passage.

Things were plenty tough for us. Lost the place in Montmartre and *The Boulevardier* folded for want of readers. But before it folded it did me a favor. I was offered a contract to go over to Hollywood and write for the new talking pictures. What a break.

And the first person I wanted to tell about it was the smart aleck Hemingway. Tell *me* how to write, would he? I could tell him something now. Universal Pictures had seen a story of mine in *The Boulevardier* and had come over five-thousand miles to sign me up. I didn't see them coming after him. Going to be the champ, was he? Well, maybe he'd find himself up against his old sparring mate in the battle of the century. You know how it is. I was dying to rub it in. Wherever he was I knew he was in there slugging. But a good boxer can always outpoint a slugger. Wait until I stick that straight Hollywood left in his kisser, I thought.

A Farewell
to Arms

I found Ernest in New York. Or rather he found
me. I was there on my way to the West Coast.
It was my first trip to the States in twelve years
and the newspapers gave me quite a write-up.
Pictures in the paper and everything. He saw it
and came around to the Plaza to see me. I was
glad he had seen it.

He looked pretty low, I thought. But that
awful Depression and the Prohibition stuff was
enough to make anybody low. He had a clean
shave though and didn't need a haircut. He even
had a tie on. He never felt right in city clothes.
Looked like a fireman out of uniform. Kept shaking his head sadly. I expected him to start con-
gratulating me. But he didn't. Guess the Depression must have caught up with him over here.

Too bad. Out of the frying pan into the fire, I thought.

"Hello," I said aloud.

"Hello," he said.

"Get some bad news?" I said.

"Yes," he said.

"About a book or something," I said.

"No," he said. "About you. Is it true?"

"Is what true?" I said.

"That you are only getting five hundred?" he said.

There he goes again, I thought. Only five hundred he says. You'd think five hundred a week was peanuts to hear him talk. Looked like he was going to break out crying, I poured him a drink of twelve-dollar Scotch fast. I knew he wouldn't let any tears dilute that. Bet he hasn't had any Scotch that good since he's been in New York, I thought.

"It's coming in every week," I said.

"Tear up your contract," he said.

"Why," he said.

"The place is a graveyard for writers getting small dough," he said.

Still thinking about graveyards, I thought. I knew it wasn't sour grapes. Just a state of mind. You could see he really felt sorry for me.

"Ever been there?" I said.

"No," he said.

"Oh," I said.

"Refused four times that much last week," he said.

"Pretty good purse for a club fighter," I said. "Suppose I could get you a good bout out there. What would you really take?"

"Ten thousand," he said.

"A year?" I said.

"A week," he said.

"Oh," I said.

What are you going to do with a guy like that, I thought. Who ever heard of a writer getting ten grand a week? That's a half million a year. Must be kidding me. If I can get him a job in Hollywood I'll do it, I thought.

I said aloud, "How is the Depression hitting you?"

"What Depression?" he said.

"I wouldn't know," I said. "Heard things were pretty tough."

"Haven't noticed it," he said. "My last bout drew a big gate. Best seller. Bought a boat and a house in Key West. I'll be shooting at the New York State title in the Garden in my next fight."

I rang up for some ice and some set-ups and when the bellboy came in with the ice he turned the knife. Held out a pencil and asked Ernest for an autograph. I reached for the pencil thinking the kid had made a mistake. I was the visiting celebrity. But the bellboy held on to the pencil and handed me the ice instead. "It's Mr. Hemingway's autograph I want," he said. "I can sell it for ten bucks anytime."

That's a hot one, I thought. Must be a gag.

"That your son, Ernest?" I said.

"Could be," he said.

The bellboy said, "I read *A Farewell to Arms* and it's a swell book."

"I've heard it well spoken of," Ernest said.

"So have we," my friends said.

"I must remember to read it," I said.

"You won't," Hemingway said.

I said farewell to New York the next day. A brass band met me at the station in Hollywood and escorted me in state to the studio. Then they forgot all about me. I couldn't learn the language. They would ask me how much I was getting and then stop speaking to me. I met an old newspaper pal of mine from Chicago named Charlie MacArthur. He was getting two grand a week, he told me. I didn't believe him until he showed me his contract. When he heard what I was getting he shook hands warmly with me. "Goodby, pal," he said. "Nice seeing you." And he walked away. That guy Hemingway must be psychic, I thought. When I saw one of the movies they made of my stuff I hit out for Paris. Couldn't take it.

I tried to contact Ernest in New York but he was fishing in Key West. After three weeks in Paris I got another offer from Hollywood. The Fox studio wanted me for a Paris picture. They didn't know I had ever been in Hollywood. I raised the ante a little this time but it still was not enough. Again I looked for Ernest. But he was still fishing.

But back in Hollywood this time I got my chance to pay him back for that big favor he had done at the Paris fights. I was working at MGM at the time. It was about a year later. I had not heard how he was doing. In Hollywood you never read or talk about anybody but yourself.

But somebody at MGM must have broken the rule. They had seen an item in O. O. Mc-Intyre's column about Hemingway and me. I was right there on the lot so they sent for me. I was escorted with great deference into Louis B. Mayer's office. Did I know Hemingway? Sure I did. Could I get him to come out to Hollywood? Sure I could—for big money. How much would he want? Plenty.

Naturally I knew that ten grand a week

was ridiculous and I also knew that Frances Marion was the highest-paid writer on the lot at that moment. She was getting $2750 a week. So I told them they would have to pay him five thousand. No harm in asking, I thought.

They never batted an eye. You'd think it was five cents the way they agreed. I couldn't wait to get out of there to send him a telegram. Here it is:

ERNEST HEMINGWAY
KEY WEST FLORIDA
   GOT YOU OFFER FIVE THOUSAND A WEEK STOP MGM STUDIO STOP THREE MONTHS CONTRACT STOP WIRE ACCEPT-ANCE STOP CONGRATULATIONS

JED

Well, I thought, it will be nice seeing the old boy again. Five grand a week! Some stipend. I knew that he wasn't the kind of guy to stop talking to an old pal just because he was in the big sugar. Nice kind of a guy to have around to put the bite on now and then too. He'd never miss it. Makes a fellow feel good to help out an old pal. I felt swell and could hardly wait for his wire. Maybe we could get a house together in Beverly Hills with a big swimming pool and everything. I was wondering how long it would take him to get there when his wire came:

JED KILEY

MGM STUDIOS

CULVER CITY CALIFORNIA

DONT BE SILLY STOP

ERNEST

There it was in black and white. I saved the telegram in case some psychiatrist in Key West might want to see it some day. How do you get that way? I thought. Five grand a week is twice as much as the President of the United States gets. And he says don't be silly. Why, F. Scott Fitzgerald was only getting a thousand on the same lot. I told Scott about it. He shook his head sadly.

"Maybe he's right," Scott said. "I heard he just turned down fifty thousand for the movie rights to *A Farewell To Arms*. Said he wants a hundred grand or nothing."

"What?" I said.

"That's right," Scott said. "And to think that I thought I was overpaid when they offered me ten for one of mine."

"He's not a writer," I said. "He's a business man."

57

"No," Scott said. "He is a great writer. If I didn't think so I wouldn't have tried to kill him that time."

"Kill him?" I said.

"Sure," Scott said. "I was the champ and when I read his stuff I knew he had something. So I dropped a heavy glass skylight on his head at a drinking party. But you can't kill the guy. He's not human."

"Hurt him much?" I said.

"Not enough," Scott said. "Only twelve stitches."

"Too bad," I said.

I could have dropped a whole roof on him after that telegram. I was counting on a nice ten per cent for getting him the job. Felt sorry for poor Scott too. Hollywood turned out to be a graveyard for him all right. He died soon after.

I left Hollywood in 1934. It was too lonely. Then one day in New York I saw a big headline in *Variety*. "HEMINGWAY GETS 100 G's FOR FAREWELL," it read. What do you know? I thought. He got it. That was tops in those days for movie rights to a novel. One hundred thousand smackers! Some purse.

Wonder if he can take it, I thought. Prosperity is harder to take than poverty. A lot of good men slow down when they get into the big money. Look at poor Scott Fitzgerald. He was a great champ until he started getting what he thought was big money. Then he never wrote another thing. The big time killed him. He was already punch drunk when I saw him in Hollywood. A has-been at thirty-five.

Wonder if Ernest will keep slugging like he always said, or get out of shape too? Might even go high-hat. I didn't see how he could get a swell-head. He had that, as big as it could stretch, ten years ago. Before he had a dime. He can dish it out, I thought, but can he take it?

I found out in the spring of '36.

Winner
Take Nothing

FLOYD Gibbons and I were down in Florida in the spring of '36. Gib was another former Chicago reporter who had made the big time. He was dragging down three grand a week for talking fast on the radio. He had a swell motor yacht called *Adventurer*. One day we cruised down from Miami to Key West.

The overseas highway that connects up the Florida Keys had not yet been built. Key West was still an island. You had to go there by water. So Ernest had his island home and his boat just like he had said he was going to have ten years before in Paris. Some fortuneteller. I was anxious to see his boat. Bet it's a honey, now that he has the dough, I thought.

We tied up at the fishing docks on the Gulf and the old *Adventurer* stood out like the

Queen Mary; all brass and gleaming white, among the local fishing craft. And the first thing we did was to ask where we could find Hemingway.

"God only knows," the dockmaster said. "We got a lot of bars in this town. His boat's *Pilar,* but he's not aboard."

So we went up to the La Concha Hotel. They've got a good bar there. But the bartender seemed nervous. He looked around carefully and lowered his voice. "Mr. Hemingway never comes in here," he said.

That's funny, I thought. Looks like the nicest place in town.

"Where can we find him?" Gib asked.

"I don't know where you can find him," the barkeep said, "but any taxi can take you to his house."

So we grabbed a cab and sure enough the driver knew just where it was. He kept looking at us in the mirror as we circled through the narrow streets. We finally stopped in front of an eight-foot stone wall with forbidding looking iron gates. The place looked like a medieval fortress. The only thing missing was the moat. The grounds covered a square block in the most thickly populated part of the town and the walls were on all four sides, with broken bottles on top to keep you from climbing over. I knew who had furnished the bottles all right.

Looking through the iron gate all you could see were palm trees set close together with a glimpse of an ancient mansion in the middle. It was a bright sunny day outside, but inside those walls it was black as night and the few pieces of ground you could see between the dense trees looked damp and mysterious. Bet there's a lot of pirate bones buried there, I thought.

When Gib pulled the bell cord by the gate a mournful dirge could be heard in the distance. It sounded like that lone church bell they ring in Spain for the dead. We waited a bit but not a sound came from the house. We rang it again and again. But nobody came to the door. That is, nobody in that house came to the door. But across the street every door in the block opened to pour out women and kids. They all stood silently watching us. The houses were mostly small unpainted shacks tied down with wires against the hurricanes. The scene reminded you of the old châteaux you see in Europe with the huts of the peasants grouped around the Monseigneur's castle for protection. The neighbors themselves looked like they had just stepped out of old paintings. The kids were mostly naked and the women wore brightly colored shawls over their heads like you see in small towns in southern Spain today or maybe Cuba. Gib cupped his hands over

63

his mouth and gave them that fast radio line of his.

"Hello everybody," he said. "Is Mr. Hemingway in town?"

Nobody answered. Nobody even moved. They just stared. The driver called out in Spanish and a couple of them nodded. But nobody said anything. The lord of the manor has them well trained, I thought. He's probably peeking out of some hidden window in his bastion right now. Dodging us the way he dodged me that day in his house by the cemetery. Some isolationist.

Still running true to form, I thought. He lives in a cemetery in Paris and in a tomb in Key West. The driver told us the place was all modern inside and a show place of the town. But try and get in. We rang the death knell again but got only a dismal echo.

Anyway we knew he was in town. So we told the driver to take us any place he might be. That was a bigger order than we thought. We must have hit twenty bars in an hour. We started at the Ocean end of Duval Street. That's the Broadway of Key West. It runs from the Ocean to the Gulf and is only about a mile long. But in that miracle mile there are more bars than you will find in two miles on Broadway. Every other store is one. We didn't go into them all;

ust the ones with sawdust on the floor. I asked
he driver why and he explained.

He said. "The Señor Hemingway is very
democratic. He does not wear the shoes when he
visit the bar. Perhaps he like the feel of the sawdust on the bare feet. Who knows?"

Barefooted, I thought. What next? You'd
think that it would have made it easier to find
him. But it didn't. The Conchs—that's what they
call the natives on the Keys—go barefooted too.
Anyway in every spot we visited it was the same
tory. We would ask for Señor Hemingway and
everybody would clam up. You could tell they all
new him. But they just weren't talking.

"They think you the police," our driver
explained.

"What's the trouble?" Gib said.

"*Quién sabe?*" the driver said. But he
ooked like he did know.

We finally hit the last joint on the street.
The driver refused to go in with us this time.
You couldn't blame him, I thought. It sure looked
plenty tough. Had a kind of stockade all around
it with a lot of gaudy posters of Cuban belly
dancers all over the unpainted front. It backed
ight up on the Gulf, and Gib said that's how
hey got rid of the bodies. Just tossed them over
he fence to the sharks. It was strictly a night

65

joint, you could see. And you know how awfu
those joints look in the daytime. It had a Spanish
name but we called it the Bucket of Blood.

We started in the door but a large dusky
gentleman with a handle-bar mustache and a
dirty apron suddenly barred the way. His huge
body filled the doorway. "No open. Come to
night," he said. But when we asked the usual
question about Hemingway a strange thing hap
pened. Instead of clamming up like the rest of
them he stood aside and bowed us in.

And you should have seen the interior of
the joint. It looked like a hurricane had hit it
Broken glass and broken chairs littered the floor
A couple of tough looking Conchs were cleaning
it up. Our host, with amazing agility for such a
big man, vaulted over the bar and came up with
a bottle of good Scotch. The best we had had in
Key West. I noticed the bar mirror over his head
was broken in two places. There were no cus
tomers and, in an unbroken spot on the mirror
I could see the two Conchs leaning on their
brooms and staring at us. The big man, you could
see, was the boss. He smiled ingratiatingly and
announced that the drinks were on the house.

"Is it that the Señor Hemingway is a fran
to you?" he said.

Oh, oh, I thought. There's something
screwy about this. I didn't like the way he wa

playing up to us. Better say we don't even know Ernest. Maybe our barefoot boy has been playing rough in the joint. I was going to warn Gib but he admitted that the Señor was our good friend before I could tip him off. Our host's next remark nearly floored us. He was a very, very tough-looking hombre.

"Please, please," he said, with his hands together as though he were praying. "Please tell your good fran' to come no more to my place. Look what happen las' night. I am afraid."

Better take the ball away from Gib, I thought. After all I had had a place of my own and knew how to talk to the guy.

"Don't worry about Señor Hemingway," I said. "He can take care of himself."

"I am not afraid *for* him," he answered, "I am afraid *of* him. *I am afraid he will hurt somebody in my place.*"

Get a load of that, I thought. The tough owner of the toughest joint in town was afraid Ernest might hurt one of his customers? Some barefoot boy!

I ordered another drink. This we gotta hear, I thought.

"Was he hurt?" I said.

"No, no," he said, "the Señor never get hurt."

"Start it?"

67

"No, no," he said, "he no start trouble. He just finish it. He win."

Winner take nothing, I thought. That's the title of one of his books. But the story I heard that day in the Bucket of Blood was a lot better than the book, in my opinion. We got it straight from the horse's mouth too; from the owner of the joint. And night-club owners don't lie.

It seems that the Señor H. had dropped in alone to the establishment about four A.M. He had just wrapped up a book and, as usual on those festive occasions, was wearing his bare feet and what he calls his "drinking shorts." That's all he had on. He enjoys hobnobbing with the key-hopping waterfront Conchs who consider shirts and shoes an affectation. They know him and they like him.

But, it appears, there were three (3) largish rumrunners out of Nassau who did not know him and who did not like his looks. They had been imbibing some of their own poison and resented the Señor's bare feet and unshaven features. The Señor only grinned at their verbal insults.

But, it seems that La Belle Conchita, who does the star strip tease according to the posters, precipitated matters innocently by tossing the Señor a rose. The gesture was resented by the rumrunners. One of them playfully broke his glass on the edge of the bar and, while retaining the jagged stem as a weapon of sorts, he had laughingly tossed the small pieces of glass under the Señor's bare feet.

That's when the trouble started. When the Señor stepped on one of them. "And," our host said, "you never see a big man move so fas' in all your life. Bottles, chairs, and tables fly around him like the rain. The furniture miss him. His punches, they do not miss."

It had all ended as quickly as it had begun, we learned, with the three rumrunners going by air through the front door, which, by the looks of it, must have been closed at the time. The Señor won by three KOs. But he paid for everything. Winner take nothing.

No wonder we couldn't find him around town. He was waiting for the heat to cool down. Afraid somebody might want to congratulate him or something. That's why he wasn't home either. Better get out of here ourselves, I thought.

We got out of there fast. You could tell the driver was relieved to see us on our feet. He knew about it all right. Just wasn't talking. Gib thought we ought to take a little run in the yacht to get the morning-after smell of the joint out of our lungs. So we headed for the dock.

The *Adventurer* sure looked clean and inviting. Wonder if we will ever see Ernest, I thought. I knew he hadn't gone to bed. All that excitement would keep anybody up. Besides, sleep wasn't very important to him. Working or playing he liked to stay awake for days. I was sorry we had missed him. So was Gib.

We got on board and were all set to pull out when the Coast Guard started running up small-craft warnings. That's the way it is down there. One minute the sun is shining brightly, and the next minute they are telling you to stay off the ocean. Bad weather hits fast on the Keys and a storm on the Caribbean is no joke.

We were helping the captain tie things down on deck and running out extra lines for the coming blow when a passing boat caught our eye. It was just one of those ordinary motor fishing boats you see all over the Keys but instead of running to shelter it was headed straight out to sea. There was a big man at the wheel and a Cuban boy standing beside him with a tray. The big man had a glass in his hand which the boy was filling from a bottle. The boat moving slowly on its motor was only a few feet from our bow. We looked at the man.

70

The Three
Day Blow

HE was an Old Man and he had not taken a fish in many days. That was because he had not been fishing. He had been playing. When he fished he took a fish. When he played he took a drink. You could see that he had not taken a shave or a sleep in many hours. The boy looked at him admiringly.

Everything was young about the Old Man except his eyes which were the color of seaweed which has been up too long. But they were cheerful and undefeated. The hand which held the glass had the deep, creased scars which came from handling schooners across the bars. Some of them were as old as erosions on a fishless desert. Others at his knuckles were fresh; as though he had barked them recently on the rough thwarts of a sea-going chin. There was another fresh scar on his cheekbone; as if it had been brushed lightly by a passing fist or a flying chair. His bare toes gripped the deck the way his strong fingers gripped the glass—as though somebody were going to take it away from him. When he saw us his raucous laugh broke the spell. He shut down his noisy motor and drifted alongside. It was the *Pilar*.

"Blow me down," he said, "If it ain't the adventurers. What you doing? Tying her down? You sissies afraid of getting your feet wet?"

Just like that, I thought. You don't see the guy for years and he talks like he had just seen you yesterday. Maybe he had, I thought. Through one of those hidden peekholes in the castle of his.

"Tie up and come aboard," Gib said. "Big blow coming."

"No can do," Ernest said. "Got a date in Bimini. Come on over when the naughty storm dies down and go fishing. It's only a one-bottle cruise." That's the way he measured time—by drinks. "I'll be there by noon tomorrow."

"You'll be in Davy Jones' Locker by noon," I said.

He looked at the sky and sniffed the air. The wind was rising and it was getting darker

72

every minute. He said something in Spanish and the boy turned the motor over. He pushed off and waved. "See you sissies when you get there. So long," he said. And he headed that tub of his straight for the Atlantic.

Well, I thought, he's still the same anyway. Still looking for trouble. And the big dough doesn't seem to have changed him. He looks worse than he did when he was broke. And you couldn't call that boat of his a yacht by any means. Guess he can take it all right, I thought.

"The man's crazy," the captain said.

"You can say that again," I said.

The sea around the Florida Keys is a graveyard for ships. In the old days the Key Westers made their living out of wrecks. The wind piled the ships up on the saw-toothed reefs, and the breakers did the rest. They say the natives used to put out the lights in the lighthouses when business was bad. The bones of thousands of ships lie buried in the shallow waters. The sudden storms, the shallow water, and the reefs still make them the most dangerous waters in the world.

And this was no small squall. It was the real thing. The Conch fishermen were all streaking for port before the wind. Even the birds were ganging up and heading inland the way they do when a hurricane is coming.

The island of Bimini, the captain told us, is just a speck in the Caribbean and hitting it in a spell of bad weather is like finding a needle in a haystack. Our friend, he said, would come limping back to Key West in a few days or we would never hear of him again. "You don't know these waters," he said. You don't know Hemingway, I thought.

As his boat went by the Coast Guard station a siren let loose that sounded like an air-raid signal. His was the only boat headed out to sea so it must have been for him. That ought to bring him back, I thought. But it didn't. He just stood up and waved with one hand and thumbed his nose at the station with the other. The last we saw of him was his little boat, heading straight into the weather. Then it faded out suddenly in the dark like a Hollywood cut.

The storm was a bad one. It hit us a minute later. You couldn't see your drink before your face. We grabbed a taxi and just made the La Concha. The palm trees were bowing low to us as we tore through the wind-swept streets. The cab itself felt like it was going to turn over any minute. The rain was hitting it like a fire hose.

74

It wasn't the hurricane season but it felt like one to me.

"God help the sailors on a night like this," Gib said.

"Amen," I said.

And it went on that way for three days and nights. We stayed holed up in the bar and watched it through the windows. All you could see on Duval Street was a Yank sailor now and then bucking the wind and rain in snug oilskins. Bet they were glad to be in port, I thought.

We pulled out for Bimini early in the morning of the fourth day. The wind and rain had stopped but there was a big ground swell. We asked about Ernest at the dock but he had not come back. We were worried. So I phoned the Coast Guard. When I mentioned his name a roar of laughter came back over the phone. "That guy knows those waters better than we do," a voice answered. The Dock Master did not share our fears either. "If that bird is ever lost at sea," he said, "It will be because they hanged him from a yardarm."

We glimpsed Bimini at sunset. And what a sight. It looked like a little tropical tiara set in emeralds. The natives say that Columbus landed there on his first voyage. Named it San Salvador, they say. I wouldn't know about that but I'll bet Chris wasn't any happier to sight land than we were.

Bimini is the smallest of the British Bahamas group in the West Indies. It's really two islands, but one is uninhabited. It lies about a hundred miles due east of Miami and, except for a small hotel, looked then pretty much as it did in Columbus' day. Has a population of about two hundred natives, and they live and look pretty much the same as they did in the fifteenth century except they listen to the fights and baseball on the radio. It's like one of those tropical islands you see in the movies: all coconut palms and white beach. The World Atlas gives it only a flyspeck and one line. "Bimini; a small island in the Bahamas, W.I. where Ponce de León is said to have discovered The Fountain of Youth."

I borrowed the captain's glasses and took a look. I picked up the dock, a long narrow jetty, but I couldn't see any signs of Hemingway's boat. There were about fifty natives standing on the jetty but not a white face in the lot. Must have come and gone, I thought. Hoped so anyway.

But he had not come and gone. We found that out while the natives were helping us tie up. The first thing they asked us was whether or not we had seen him. When we told them we had seen him start out for here four days ago they were all smiles. I couldn't see what was so funny about a man being out for days in a storm. But they did.

"No storm too bad for Papa," one of them said. "Storm over. He come sure now."

We hoped they were right but had our doubts. We spotted a little native bar at the foot of the jetty and headed for there. The going had been plenty tough all day and we were about ready for bed. A couple of the boys helped us walk and took us right to the bar without our telling them. Papa has them well trained, I thought. We made the bar and flopped down on a couple of bar stools. And after a few of those good Scotches you get on British islands we started to feel better.

But we were still worried about Ernest. Gib wanted to call up Key West and report him missing. They had a radio phone on Bimini and we might have done it, but if we did and he turned up safe I knew he would be sore. He always hated any publicity about his private life. Sounds funny but it's true. Ask any newspaper man who knows him. Won't even talk about his own books let alone talk about himself. You got to give the devil his due. Look what he did when I gave him a write-up in *The Boulevardier*.

So we rolled up to the hotel and went to bed instead.

Came the dawn and we got some good news. The boy who brought our coffee was all smiles. Papa's boat had been seen limping into port, he announced. He would make the jetty in an hour or so and the whole island would be there to meet him. You'd think it was Christopher Columbus coming back again, I thought.

But Gib and I were right there with the rest when the *Pilar* chugged up to dock. The boat you could see had taken a bad beating. Some storm. But Ernest looked all right from where we stood. We weren't on the jetty. There wasn't room. We waited up in front of the bar. We knew where he would head for first. And you should have seen and heard the welcome the guy got. They even had a three-piece band on hand. You'd think it was Lindbergh riding down Fifth Avenue except for the tune the band was playing. It was "God Save the King." And they were treating him like a king, too. All laughing and smiling and yelling and as glad to see him as we were.

We were right about where he would head for first. He came on a beeline for the bar grinning and pushing his way through the half-naked bodies like a conquering hero. He was half-naked too and so wind-burned he looked like one of

them. He walked in his bare feet over the nail-
and splinter-infested jetty as though it were a
thick carpet. Some feet. The soles must have been
like leather. He looked pretty tired though, I
thought. Still had his sea legs and staggered from
side to side. But he had plenty of friends to help
him along. Seemed happy as a kid to see them.
The Cuban boy who was his mate wasn't with
him. He was already in his bunk, asleep. No
wonder, after that day-and-night pounding. But
it did not seem to have hurt Ernest much, I
thought.

After
the Storm

You could see the storm hadn't hurt Ernest's
thirst. He pushed right by into the bar and
knocked off two big hookers of straight Scotch
without batting an eye. Then he shook hands and
I noticed it hadn't hurt his grip either. Those cal-
luses of his made dents in your palm. Felt like he
was holding a handful of marbles.

"How did you find the Atlantic?" I said.

"Big," he said.

"Have a nice crossing?" Floyd Gibbons
asked.

"No," he said.

"Why?" I said.

"Ran out of liquor," he said.

"That's awful," Gib said.

"How about food?" I said.

"Raw flying fish," he said.

And that's about all we could get out of him. Just the clipped dialogue he puts in those books of his. You'd think he had just come from a rowboat ride in Central Park for all we could get him to say. Some boat ride. We took a bottle over to the hotel with us and watched him wolf a big steak. It was enough for a family of four.

"What do we do to get the story of the storm," Gib said, "wait for you to write it and then buy it?"

"No story," he said. "Just ran out a sea anchor and rode out the blow."

"Oh," I said.

"Like a tough fight," he said. "You just keep your head down and hang on."

"How about that fight on Duval Street?" I said.

"What fight?" he said.

Most fellows like to talk about their bar-room battles. I keep telling the same ones over and over to the same people. Get a kick out of it. But you couldn't get the guy to open up. Most people who drink get gabby. But he got cagier with each shot. No use trying to feed him a lot of drinks to get him to talk. You wound up by telling *him* how you licked that big guy the other night.

While we were still in the dining room we

had a couple of visitors. Here comes the floor show, I thought. They think of everything for this bird. But he warned us not to laugh. This was serious business. One of the visitors you could see was a person of some importance on the island. He was wearing a silk opera hat and tails. The question of white or black tie, I noticed, he had handled with great tact. He wore neither. In fact, he wore no shirt. His bare feet were the conventional black.

The other native wore nothing but red walking shorts. And what a build! He looked like a composite picture of Max Baer and Joe Louis. Stood about six-two and had long, powerful arms that hung to his knees. Some reach. And you could see the long, lithe muscles rippling like snakes when he moved. He walked like a tiger and looked about twenty-one.

As they got to our table the one in the silk hat swept it off with a graceful gesture and crushed it flat against his chest. He spoke with an Oxford accent. "My compliments, gentlemen," he said. "I am here to present the challenge of Mr. Disraeli."

Gib and I just looked at each other. We couldn't figure out what the big idea could be. Sounded like a duel. But Ernest probably knew. He bowed in return.

83

"OK," he said, "get the gloves and the ring ready; I'll be out in two drinks."

Silk Hat Harry snapped his topper open with a ducal gesture and the two of them walked out as quietly as they had come. We turned to Ernest for an explanation. He seemed a little self-conscious, I thought.

"I have a standing offer of ten pounds," he said, "to any native who can stay two rounds with me, and Dizzy wants to take a chance. That's all."

"That's all?" Gib said. "You don't mean to tell me you're going to box that big guy now?"

"Why not?" Ernest said.

"You're not in condition," Gib said.

"Put it off until tomorrow," I said.

"I can't," he said. "They've been waiting for me all week. Told them when I left for Key West that I would take him on when I got back. I'm back now and I don't want to lose face."

"You'll lose your face if you do," I said.

"Don't be silly," he said.

How crazy can a guy get? I thought. He is thirty-five years old, has been fighting the elements four days on raw fish, no sleep, and salt water; and now he is going to fight a man bigger and younger than he is, right after eating. I might have bet on him if he had been in shape but he didn't even have his land legs yet. Better try again to stop him.

"You can't go two rounds," I said.

"Any bets?" he said.

"No," I said. What's the use, I thought. It's his funeral. You can't tell the guy anything about his writing or his fighting anyway.

After we had had a few more highballs he picked up a little hand bell from the table and handed it to me. "You be the referee, timekeeper, and judge," he said. "You won't have much to do. Don't count him out too fast, though. I always give them a long count. And don't pull us apart if we clinch. You might get hurt. If he bites me don't disqualify him. I'll bite him back. Watch the time carefully and ring the bell when three minutes is up. If he is still on his feet after two rounds he wins."

Some confidence, I thought. Losing never seemed to enter his mind. He felt the same about his fighting as he did about his writing. If he lost the first round he would get his knockout in the second. Hope he can fight better than he can write. He handed me ten dollars.

"This for me?" I said.

"That's the loser's purse," he said. "Slip it to him right after the fight." How do you like that? Some gall.

As we walked out of the hotel a cheer went up from the beach that could have been heard in Miami. They cheered in the English fashion, "Hip, hip, hur*rah!*" I've seen a lot of fights in my time but never an audience like that. Everybody on the island must have been there. They were all standing on the beach in the form of a ring. The inside row—the boys in the ringside seats—were holding hands in a circle to keep the others back. That's the way they did in old England when prize fighting first started. That's why they still call our square boxing arenas "rings" I guess.

The ring looked just about the right size. Not having any ropes but the natives' arms it was flexible of course. But that was all right with me. It would be harder for Dizzy to get my man on the ropes.

As we elbowed our way through the cheering crowd you could see Papa was the favorite. He might have been a home-town hopeful fighting in his own club from the way they treated him. You could see he loved it too. Always wanted to be the champ and was getting a kick out of it. He looked like Dempsey going into the ring, only he had more hair on his chest—and more belly.

When we got to the ring the boys who

were the posts raised their clasped hands and we went under them like children playing London Bridge. But when I saw the professional gloves they were using I knew it wasn't any child's play. This was for keeps.

As they put on the gloves I sized up the two of them. And I didn't feel as confident as Ernest did. Kid Disraeli, in the red trunks, was at least ten years younger and ten pounds heavier. He had a longer reach and smaller belly. But, as I say, it wasn't my funeral. I picked up a couple of coconuts and tossed them out of the ring. A fighter in his bare feet could break a toe on a coconut. I looked up on the porch and there was Gib in a rocking chair. He had an upper box seat and was laughing. I wished I had stayed up there with him. It was going to be tough keeping out of the way of these heavyweights in that soft sand.

I sat down in the sand to wait and got right up again. Talk about the hot seat. It was like sitting on a red-hot stove. How they could stand it in their bare feet, let alone fight in it, had me puzzled. But Ernest didn't seem to notice it at all. The soles of his feet are like Neolite or something. Bet he could walk on hot coals like those Indian fakirs.

When they were ready I called both fighters to the center of the ring for instruction the way they do at the Garden, but both boys stayed in their "corners." "We got our own rules," Hemingway said. "Just ring that bell and get out of range."

I announced the fight as being for the championship of Bimini and got a rousing cheer. Then I glanced at my wrist watch and rang my little bell.

At the sound of the bell the giant in the red trunks came out of his corner like a bounding rhino. He came out slugging and you could see he had a haymaker in either hand. One sock, I thought, and the Old Man of the Sea is going to be ship wrecked again. But they were not landing. The boy in the light skin was making him miss, he was moving gracefully to one side or the other like those bullfighters in his books. Then just when I thought he was going to get gored he got on his bicycle. How a man his size could move so fast with a metal kneecap and in the soft sand had me puzzled. I was having an awful time just keeping out of the way. My shoes were full of sand and I was panting more than they were. The round must be about over, I thought, but I was afraid to look at my watch. Might get clipped.

Up until now Hemingway had not let one

punch go. Stalling the first two minutes, I thought. He will probably go in now and slug out the last minute, like he said. But he didn't. The challenger rushed him again and this time got him right up against the living ropes and let go a roundhouse right that would have knocked the champ's head off if it had hit him. But it didn't hit him. He ducked and two of the ring posts dropped in their tracks instead. Some reach. As referee I didn't know what to do. But the spectators did. Two new posts just moved in, clasped hands, and the ring was whole again. Apparently it had happened before.

The incident gave me time to glance at my watch. Holy Moses, the round had lasted four minutes. I rang the bell and the round was over. The fighters didn't go to their corners. There were no corners to go to. They just laid down in the sand and shaded their eyes from the sun. That sun is going to win over me by a knockout any minute, I thought. The crowd went wild. This was the first time a native had ever stayed a whole round, I learned later.

One of the waiters from the bar was next to Ernest. Looked like a real fight second too. He was giving Ernest the water bottle like they do at the pro fights to rinse out the mouth. I needed it as much as he did so I grabbed a swig from the bottle and nearly choked to death. Scotch on the rocks! No wonder he didn't spit it out. I didn't either.

I glanced over at the challenger's corner and got a shock. Red trunks was up on his feet shadow boxing! That extra minute of fighting hadn't even warmed him up. Wasn't even breathing hard. The minute of rest was up, but I decided to play fair and give Ernest and me another minute's rest. Papa was flat on his back and you could see his belly rising and falling like a heavy ground swell. I thought he was asleep. But he was up on his feet with his guard up before you knew it. Pure instinct, I guess. Wonder why he ever took up writing. Could have been champion of the world and then opened a bar. Like those other champs.

As I rang the bell for the second round, a shadow seemed to pass over the sun and a gust of hot wind hit me. I thought it was one of those sudden storms you get in the Caribbean. But it was just the dark cloud in the red trunks rushing by me for the kill. Talk about your Hurricane Jacksons; this guy was Hurricane Edna, Carol, and Connie all in one! Went by me like a windmill on skis. You could hear the spars whistling as he headed Sou-by-Sou-West straight for the target. Here's where he lowers the boom on our Key West sailor, I thought. I'm going to be saying "the winnah and *new* champion" any second.

But the Old Man of the Sea just swayed with the wind like a storm-wise palm tree. His big feet were in the sand; those prehensile toes of his were holding on like the roots of a palm. Ever see the palm trees dig in during a big blow? You can tell they're just waiting for a lull; bending not bowing. I've seen coconuts flying through the air in Florida fall hurricanes like baseballs in spring practice. But I've never seen one man dodge so many in so short a time. They were coming at Papa from all directions at once. But that palm-tree, bullfighter technique of his never changed. Too bad he didn't have one of those red capes to hide behind, I thought.

Then the full center of the storm struck. Thunder and lightning and all. The dark cloud thundered in close with everything he had. He was smelling victory now and throwing caution to the winds. You could see that pile-driver right of his starting from the sand. His fist looked like the iron ball they use for wrecking buildings back home. Here it comes now, I thought.

And it did come. But not the way I thought. A streak of left-handed white lightning

suddenly buried itself in the dark cloud's middle. You couldn't see from what direction it had
come but you could see it had struck hard.

Ever see a bull fall when he gets that
final straight right to the heart? That's the way
this one fell, slowly, like he was tired. Went to
his knees, like he was saying his prayers. Then
he turned over and went to sleep.

Didn't even have to count. But I did. Gave
him the long Chicago count. But he never stirred.
The man in the light skin had won by a knockout in the first ten seconds of the second round.
I grabbed his big hand and held it up the way
they do at the Garden. He was panting so hard
he nearly blew me over.

"The winnah and still champion: *Papa!*"
I announced.

"Cut that out and come up to the bar," he
said. I couldn't have gone anywhere else if I
wanted to. In a second everybody had broken
the circle and headed for the bar. I was carried
along in the crush of cheering, yelling fight fans.
They filled the bar and overflowed on to the
jetty. Must be a regular ritual, I thought. But
they didn't look like fight fans. They looked more
like kids just out of school.

And the biggest kid of them all was Hemingway. He showed them how he let go that

92

right while the four extra bartenders were passing out soft drinks. I noticed *he* wasn't drinking a soft drink. They could have anything they liked, he told me, but they liked the sweet stuff. I got a Scotch. I asked him if it was a legal holiday on the island. Nobody was working.

"Every day is a holiday here," he said, "unless you call fishing work."

While we were standing there the loser came in and got a big hand. They opened up a path for him to the bar. He was still a little wobbly but he ordered a root beer. I slipped him the ten spot and he thanked me politely.

"My word," he said, "what happened?"

"You forget to duck," Ernest said.

Gib and I got a great kick out of the big bruiser saying "My word" and drinking root beer through a straw. Maybe he's not so tough after all, I thought. You know how it is. When you see a guy knocked cold he does not look so tough afterwards. And you get sore at the guy who hit him too.

Ernest must have read my mind. "How did you like the fight?" he said.

"Too one-sided," I said, "and a little sadistic. You didn't have to hit the poor palooka so hard."

That ought to burn him up, I thought.

93

But it didn't seem to. He just put his arm around me and hissed in my ear:

"Bet you a thousand bucks to a hundred you can't stay two rounds with him right now," he said.

That's a lot of dough. A thousand for only six minutes' work. I glanced over at the loser. Those kids recover fast, I thought.

"Don't be silly," I said.

"Time for my siesta," he said and headed for the hotel. That was around noon, and we did not see him again the rest of the day or night. About eighteen hours' straight sleep. Some siesta.

Men
Without Women

ONE morning, just as the sun also rose, Ernest was pounding on our door. Floyd Gibbons and I wanted to sleep. But try and do it. If you didn't let him in he would break the door down. Never saw a man with such energy in all my life. It was May and we were in the tropics where everybody takes it easy. But that's not the Hemingway of life. He wants action wherever he is. And he gets it. So we got up and went fishing.

We took Gib's boat, Ernest's tackle. There were five of us men without women; the captain, the three of us and a native bait-cutter. Ernest tried to get his Cuban mate to come along but the boy had more sense. He was tired after that storm session and you can't blame him. Said he wanted to see that the rudder was repaired and stayed in bed.

As you head out to sea from the Bimini jetty you pass the partly submerged wreck of a big steel freighter. Gib thought it would be a pretty good spot to fish and so did I. But Ernest had other ideas.

"Where do you think you are?" he said. "In Lake Michigan! We are going after tuna, not perch."

The only way Gib and I had ever gone after tuna was in a tin can. So we went after tuna the hard way. From the time it took to get to the spot, I thought we must be going to Miami for a tuna sandwich. We were almost a full bottle out of Bimini before we slowed down. But it was a beautiful ride just the same. The sea had calmed down overnight, and the sun coming up between the palm trees on the island made it look like those colored postal cards they sell you in Miami.

Then Ernest started strapping the harness on me. It's a sort of strait-jacket affair that goes around your waist and over your shoulders and has a socket to hold the end of the fishing pole like the color sergeants in the army use to carry the flags in a parade. And you should have seen the fishing pole. It was as big around as a clothes pole and had a reel as big as a hand organ. Weighed a ton. The line wrapped around it looked more like telephone cable than fish line. There must have been miles of it from the size of the spool. And when I got a look at the bait I thought I had caught a fish already. It was the biggest one I had ever had on a line. Must have weighed over three or four pounds and it was all trussed up on a three-pronged hook that reminded you of the hooks in a meat market. Big as your fist. I thought they were kidding me. A fish hook is a little thing, like a bent pin, with a barb on it that always gets caught in your pants. I'd hate to have this one caught on my pants, I thought.

I said aloud, "What are we after, elephants?"

"This is no joking matter," Hemingway said. "That tackle set me back nine hundred bucks. If you lose it you go right overboard after it."

Then he tossed the bait over the side and went up on the flying bridge to get a bird's-eye view of the fish. Gib was sitting alongside of me to help out with a little expert advice of his own. He knew about as much about deep-sea fishing as I did, so we were even.

"I'll tell you when they are coming," Ernest said.

Can you imagine that? I thought. He's

going to tell me when the fish are coming. What's
he got? A diver's helmet? Or does he think this is
a glass-bottomed boat? Or maybe he's got an
X-ray machine up there to see a fish way down
in that dark, green water. Must have been a mile
deep where we were. Then he tells me that when
I feel something tickle the bait a little I should
slip the release and not jerk the pole but let the
line run out until I count ten. "Wait until he
swallows it," he says.

How the hell am I going to know when he
swallows it, I thought. You'd think I was the
fish's doctor out there in the water telling him to
say "Ah." Just then I saw something white about
fifty feet off the stern. I didn't feel anything but
saw something splash. Gib saw it too. "You got
him, reel in," he yelled. I jerked the pole back
so hard it beaned me on the forehead. But I had
the fish all right. Saw him jump right out of the
water. I started reeling.

"That's your bait," Ernest said. "We're
trolling on the surface."

He was right, that time anyway. I let the
line out again and could see the bait following
us like he was alive. I took a good look at him so
I'd know him the next time. A drink or two later
Ernest yelled again, "Look out. Couple of big
ones are flirting with it." Better do it his way this

time, I thought. Then I felt something. Just a slight tug on the line. That can't be a big fish, I thought. Feels like a perch nibbling. It came again. So I released the catch, let the line run out, and counted ten. Hope I'm counting that fish out the way I did Disraeli, I thought. I gave him the long count too. At twelve I snapped the catch back on and jerked that pole as hard as I could.

And then it happened. Somebody jerked back so hard the tackle and I nearly went overboard together. And you should have seen that line run out. Straight down it went toward China. In two seconds flat Ernest was beside me yelling in my ear. "Hold on. You got a quarter of a ton of fish on there. Let him sound."

I couldn't hear any sound from the fish but I held on for dear life just the same and that line kept going out so fast it started to smoke. Ernest grabbed the pitcher of ice water and poured it on the reel. "If it slackens a little, pump and reel," he said.

It did slacken a little after what seemed hours. The fish must have hit the bottom, I thought. Three quarters of the line, I could see from the reel, was straight down in the ocean, and the reel held four hundred yards of line. That meant the water was about as deep as the Empire State Building is tall. All I had to do now

was to pull that fish up again. And if you ask
me, I'd rather climb the steps of the Empire State
Building, step by step, any time.

The reeling wasn't so hard. It was geared
down a lot. But pumping with the left was
murder. I stood it as long as I could and then
threw in the sponge. They say it was twenty-five
minutes. My arm hurt so I could hardly get out
of the harness. While I was wriggling out and
groaning Hemingway took the pole and with
those big feet of his gripping the deck, played
that whale—or whatever it was—like a brook
fisherman playing a trout. I watched him for half
an hour. Then it seemed to get easier. He was
pumping and reeling like a steam engine. What
a left.

"Sharks are after him," he said.

There he goes again with that fortune-
telling stuff, I thought. The fish is still a hundred
feet down in the ocean and he tells us the sharks
are biting him. Better go after him while his
hands are busy, I thought. Gib must have been
thinking the same thing.

"How do *you* know?" he said.

I said aloud, "Why it's very simple, Gib,
Mr. Hemingway and Mr. Fish have a sort of
Morse code between them. The fish taps out an

SOS over that telegraph line in his mouth, and Mr. H receives it over the line in his hands."

"That's right," Ernest said.

And he went on pumping and reeling like a madman. You could see it was a lot easier than when I had the pole. The line was coming in now almost as fast as it went out. I started pouring ice water on it as a gag and got a kick in the shins for my trouble. Imagine kicking anybody with bare toes. I wouldn't kick a pillow with that ingrown toenail of mine. The guy has concrete toes like a statue, I thought. Hurt me more than it did him.

Then things really started to happen. He had the fish so close to the surface you could see him. It was a tuna all right and what a tuna. Looked like a whale and he wasn't alone. There were three or four other guys as big as he was with him only they were charging and snapping at him like a hungry man snapping at a tuna sandwich.

Sharks and what sharks! That marine telegraph wasn't so far off after all, I thought. The captain and our bait-cutter grabbed long, wicked-looking gaffs and went into action. Gib and I went into hiding.

Sharks, they say, are no match for a big

tuna unless he's hurt or hooked, but once they get him helpless on a line it's different. The only friend the tuna had was Hemingway and the way he jerked that big fish away from those sharks was something to see. Said he was afraid the sharks would cut the line. Their skin is like rough sandpaper made of powdered glass. If one just brushes against you, you start bleeding.

You could see the poor tuna was all in when they finally got him on the winch. Somebody had taken a fifty-pound bite out of him. That must have been when he sent the wire to Hemingway, I thought. Even as they pulled him on the big winch one of the sharks jumped five feet out of the water and took a bite out of him as though he were cheese. You could hear the shark's teeth snap like a steel trap. Some teeth. Some tuna too. He was ten feet long and must have weighed five hundred pounds even with the bites out of him.

I felt pretty good about my catch. After all I had hooked him first. The bait-cutter brought us a round of drinks to celebrate. But Hemingway was sore. He took his drink but said he hated sharks. The bait-cutter hated them too. Kept shaking his fist at the water. Who doesn't hate sharks, I thought. You could see them hanging around the boat watching us to see if we were going to throw out another line. It gave you cold shivers just to look at them. But Papa Hemingway fooled them.

"No use fishing around here any more," he said. "I'll show you landlubbers some real he-man sport. We will go back and get the tools. We've got five hundred pounds of bait and from now on we're after sharks."

Well, I thought, you would certainly need a pretty big hook to carry that tuna as bait and a telegraph pole to fish with, not to mention a two-inch hawser for a line. But I didn't say anything. When you are fishing with Hemingway you don't say much. He doesn't either.

But on the way back he told us his father had given him a fishing pole for his birthday when he was only two years old and a double-barreled shotgun when he was ten.

The trip back was relaxing. Except for the blood all over the deck you'd have thought we were just sitting around in some quiet bar. And you should have seen Papa that day. Naked, except for a pair of blood-stained shorts, with a stubble on his chin just long enough to look untidy. A tuna is a red-blooded fish and he had so much blood on him he might have been a tuna himself. You'd certainly never take him for a writer. I never did anyway, I thought.

103

I said aloud, "What's this I hear about your telling *Who's Who* that your favorite sports were fishing, hunting, and drinking?"

"That's right," he said, "but they changed it to 'fishing, hunting, and *reading.*' "

"Hear you got a hundred grand for the rights to *Farewell to Arms,*" I said.

"That's all," he said. "Should have asked two hundred."

That's all, I thought. Where does he get that stuff? You'd think a hundred grand was peanuts. That was too much for Gib. He went below to take a nap. I was plenty tired too. The sea and the sun and the excitement get you tired when you are out with Ernest. But he was full of pep. Started cleaning his tackle while we chatted. You could see he loved it. And he breathed in that sea air like an old tar.

"How did you like the picture?" I said aloud.

"What picture?" he said.

"Farewell," I said.

"Didn't see it," he said.

"What?" I said. "You didn't see your own picture?"

"That's right," he said.

"Why?" I said.

"Why should I?" he said. "If you go out

there they get you writing as though you were looking through a camera lens. All you think about is pictures when you ought to be thinking about people. You've got to live the life of your characters to write about them."

There's the guy's secret, I thought; living the life of his characters. That's why he was running around with the Countess in Paris that time. He didn't care anything about her. He just stuck a pin in her like those butterfly collectors do. Wanted to see what made her tick. The guy, I realized for the first time, is a perfectionist. That's what he is. Whether or not you like his style of writing doesn't mean a thing. The point is he knows *what* he is writing about and *you* know it. He's not a fiction writer. He's a reporter of emotions. And he never writes about any emotion he has not experienced himself.

Take *A Farewell to Arms*. It's about the Italian Army. Well, he ought to know something about that. He got himself shot up in the Italian Army, didn't he? They say his stuff is full of tragedy. So what? He lived across from the cemetery long enough to know about death. And how about that tomblike house he has in Key West. Maybe that's why he lives there. And he has been courting death himself enough to know just how it feels when your number is up. Going

105

out in that storm in that little boat of his showed the guy's curiosity about danger. And look at him going up against those three rumrunners in the Bucket of Blood. Bet he felt like running out of the joint when the fight started. But he didn't run because the desire to learn how it feels to be on the spot was the stronger urge. Wanted to feel it so he could write about it some day. Living the life of his characters is the guy's trade. *To Have and Have Not,* they tell me, was a book about a tough guy just like the one who broke the glass off in that very fight. He just used the guy as a guinea pig.

Look at *Death in the Afternoon.* You look at it. I don't want to. But let me tell you something. That's the one about Spanish bullfighters, and they tell me the guy lived with a bullfighter to learn about bullfighting from him. Not only that, he learned to fight the bull himself. He actually got out there in the arena and *fought* a bull. They say he got gored pretty badly too. And what did he do it for? I'll tell you. He got himself kicked in the pants by the bull so he could find out first hand just how those matadors, or whatever they call them, feel about it themselves. He is a guy who wants to learn about it right from the bull's mouth.

Take *Across the River and into the Trees.*

And you can take that one too if you want to. I wouldn't stand in your way. As a matter of fact, I thought it was the Civil War story about Stonewall Jackson when he got shot. But they tell me it has a lot of Hemingway's own character in it. Sort of a psychoanalysis of himself between the lines. Mirror-writing I guess they call it. I can't read that stuff to save my life. But it just goes to show you.

Take one of his early short stories. Take 'em all if you want to. The one I mean is "The Snows of Kilimanjaro." Get a load of that title. You'd think it was about winter sports, wouldn't you? I did. You know, ski-jumping in the Swiss Alps or something. Well, get out your fan. It's about Africa. No kidding. And who the hell ever heard of snow in Africa? I didn't notice Bogart wearing ear muffs and mittens in *The African Queen.* Did you? I thought he had on a sun helmet and shorts. Must be my eyes. Ever see a safari on snowshoes in a Martin Johnson film? Or Frank Buck skating after a polar bear in the Sahara? It just goes to show you, I say.

Let's look into the significance of that screwy word Kill-a-man-jaro. Why, its nothing but the old cemetery influence working again and again and again. Death never takes a holiday with that guy. Always killing somebody. You know, some people think because they kill a lot of guys they are great writers—like Shakespeare or Jack Webb. But I don't see these two letting their characters die in bed the way *he* does in "The Killers" and "The Snows." Hamlet and his friend Macbeth didn't take it lying down. They were in there in the last round slugging it out with knives and poison. What's new about a guy dying in bed? If you ask me, the *author* should have stood in bed. I say, let this bird Jaro, or whatever his name is, die with his boots on. But try and tell *him* that!

Let's skip quickly over *Green Hills of Africa*. Ever read it? I didn't. It's an old one of his. First it's *green* hills and then it's white snow—in *Africa*. It's the title that crabbed it. Look at those Foreign Legion pictures in Technicolor. Those green hills of his are *yellow* sand dunes. Must have written that one with a green fountain pen.

So much for literary criticism. Better soft-soap him now, I thought.

I said aloud, "Nice piece of reporting you did in *Death in the Afternoon*."

Something told me I should not have said it. The fellow is funny about compliments. Doesn't like them. Thinks you are yessing him.

"Forget it," he said. "That's not you talking. It's Hollywood. The minute you heard I got a hundred Gs for *Farewell* you began to think I could write. I'm no better now than I was when I lived over the cemetery. Just getting more dough. That's all."

Maybe it is like that, I thought. When you know somebody well you don't think they can be so hot. Because you know them. Then when they make good you begin to think they *must* be good. Well, I still don't think much of "The Killers." Felt like asking him what had become of *it* if it was so good. He wrote it ten years before over the cemetery but I certainly had never heard of the thing since. Bet he couldn't sell that one to the movies, I thought.

As we passed the old wreck on our way in we noticed a swank little cruiser anchored over there. So we headed over to see who our visitors were. The boat was a little honey. I was sure glad we were in the *Adventurer* instead of Ernest's boat. More class. The cruiser was lying in the lee of the wreck, and the water was as smooth as glass. It was spick and span the way a boat ought to be. You could see two fellows fishing from easy chairs in the stern. They had a table between them and each held a highball in one hand and a slender little one-handed perch-pole in the center. It was sure a swell setup. Wonder what they will say when they get a look at our blood-stained pirate, I thought.

"Some sportsmen," he said. He thought that still-fishing for pan fish was strictly for the birds unless you were doing it for bait.

The captain shut off our motors and we drifted in on them. They had not seen us as yet when one of them let out a yell. He had taken a fish. But he did not reel in. Didn't want to take the glass out of his other hand, I guess. He just jerked the toy rod and up popped a brightly colored little fish about six inches long. Instead of taking the fish off the hook he swung the pole in a wide arc like a fellow casting backwards. Then we knew why he had yelled. A grinning black face in a cook's white hat appeared at an open window in the back of him and a capable hand caught the line on the fly. A knife flashed in the sunshine. The odor of frying fish caught our nostrils.

This was too much for Hemingway. He let out a roar that brought Gib rushing up on deck. Probably thought we were sinking. The two hardy fishermen looked up and didn't even bat an eye. All three of us recognized them as Messrs. Wooly Donahue and Ben Finney, old friends and erstwhile men about towns like Paris and Palm Beach.

"Your just in time for lunch," Wooly said. "Come aboard and pick your dish."

We tied up to them and in a few minutes had been provided with easy chairs and a fresh bottle of Scotch. This is the life, I thought. Gib liked it too. No excitement. Just solid comfort. Ernest didn't like anything about it but the Scotch which was the real uncut Nassau vintage. He wouldn't even sit down. When he saw the cook baiting the hooks you could see it was almost too much for him. The bait was strips of red flannel! No fooling. Looks like the boys will be without underwear next winter, I thought.

We looked over the side. The water was about thirty or forty feet deep but you could see right to the bottom. And you could see hundreds of little fish of all colors fighting to get at that bait. You had to jerk it away from them. Ben held his flannel-baited hook out of the water.

"Which one do you want for lunch?" he asked Gib.

"I'll take the yellow one over there," Gib said. And as we watched, Ben threw his line in, jerked the hook away from three or four baby bluefish until the yellowtail bit. Took about thirty

111

seconds in all. It was like taking a fish out of one of those tanks they have in seafood restaurants in New York. Up he came over Ben's shoulder right into the waiting hands of the cook.

We had hardly ordered our dinner when there it was on the table. Quickest service you ever saw. And what fish. Ernest shook his head sadly but I noticed it didn't interfere with his appetite. Gib and I were all for making a day of it. But not Ernest. "Make a softy out of you," he said.

When we took off for shore the two sports-men were still at it. Betting ten bucks on which could take a certain fish first. Some fun.

"That's what dough does to you," Hemingway said.

"It can do it to me any time it wants to," I said.

"Me too," Gib said.

The reception was on the jetty when we docked. Any time Papa docks the whole island turns out. They pitched in and helped us get our tuna on the scales. I had my picture taken stand-ing along side of it with the harness, big tackle, our bait-cutter and everything. Some picture. Some tuna too. Weighed 520 pounds.

Ernest told the natives to help themselves.

That's enough food for a year, I thought. At least a million sandwiches. But what do you think? All they took was a small filet off the belly weighing not over a few pounds. Some waste, I thought. But Ernest explained that the meat wasn't good in the tropics at this time of the year. It seems you got to catch them up north in the cold water for canning. But he said he knew somebody who would like it.

"Who?" I said.

"The sharks," he said. "We will feed it to them with lead sauce."

Death in
the Afternoon

I began to catch on when they hooked a wooden
raft on the stern of our boat and started wiring
our tuna to the raft. Then I saw what he had
meant by "the tools." He got them out of his
boat. Some tools. One was a sawed-off repeating
shotgun that looked like a howitzer. Instead of
buckshot each shell was loaded with ten or twelve
big steel ball bearings about the size of a .45
slug. It had once belonged to gangsters and you
only had to get hit by *one* of those pellets to get
your name in the papers. The muzzle of the thing
looked like the entrance to the Holland Tunnel.
Couldn't miss with it.

The second tool was a Thompson machine
gun. It tossed out 45-caliber slugs at the rate of
600 a minute. The Tommy gun also had been
taken away from gangsters in a certain town and

presented to a certain party by the police department. No information as to the number of the "Boys" it had rubbed out was available. But it sure looked sinister. The third tool was just a Colt automatic .45 pistol. It looked like a kid's toy pistol alongside of that sawed-off shotgun. The sharks are going to have a nice little dinner party, I thought.

As we headed out to deep water, the Bimini contingent gave us a rousing cheer. Nobody hates a shark like a native does—unless it's Hemingway. The raft was following us on a towline about twenty feet long. You could see the tuna blood dripping in the water. That's like sending an invitation to dinner by telegraph to the sharks, Ernest explained. They can smell it or something a mile away. Just like we hear a dinner bell. We had plenty of ammunition with us, both liquid and solid and were looking forward to a nice afternoon of revenge.

Floyd Gibbons had the sawed-off shotgun, Ernest the Tommy gun, and I had the Colt. I'm a crack shot with a pistol, if I do say so myself. That's why I took the pistol. To show the boys some fancy shooting.

About half a bottle out, the sharks started picking up our scent. You could see their dorsal fins coming up on all sides. So we got ready to

116

welcome our guests. Ernest and Gib took their weapons with them and climbed up on the flying bridge above me. I stayed below in the stern fishing chair, pulled my yachting cap down to shield my eyes from the sun and made myself comfortable. The ring-side seat gave me an advantage, I thought. Put me just that much closer to the target. Ernest called out the battle orders to me.

"Just don't stand up," he said.

Can you imagine that, I thought. Me stand up in front of those two guys with that gangster artillery? Must think I'm crazy. I may not know much about fishing but if there is one thing I do know it's guns.

Meanwhile our guests were really gathering around. We let them follow us for a while and then slowed down to a walk. There must have been about ten of them slowly circling the raft. Casing the joint. Now and then one of the ugly brutes would roll over on his side and look us over with a cold appraising eye like those human killers in Hemingway's story. I'd sure hate to have one of them staring at me that way if I was in the water, I thought.

"Don't shoot until they start to jump," Ernest said.

The captain slowed us down so we were

just barely moving. Enough to keep the raft far enough away from the boat. I noticed the sharks traveled in twos. Took their mates right along to dinner with them. No men without women here, I thought. Then a big guy jumped. Looked like a freight train coming out of the water, and his wide-open mouth looked like a railroad tunnel with teeth. You could get your whole head in it. Some dentures too. And he must have been ten feet long.

I was so awed at the very size of the guy that I got buck ague. Forgot to shoot. Guess Gib did too. But Killer Hemingway hadn't forgotten to shoot. You could hear the Tommy gun rat-tat-tatting and actually see the tracers going right into the shark's body. He seemed to stop in mid-air for an instant at the top of his arc and then fell like a ton of bricks on the raft. The raft almost turned over from the shock and you could see blood shooting out of the bullet holes in the shark's side like red water out of faucets as he flopped back into the drink. And that was the signal for the most horrible sight you ever saw.

While the wounded shark was still flopping and very much alive the others forgot all about the tuna and turned on him. He fought back but he didn't have a chance. They tore him to pieces before our eyes. The water turned red with blood. It swirled like a red whirlpool as they fought to get at him. They had fresh meat now and you could hear their awful teeth ripping and tearing like a wrecking crew on an old building. Cannibals and what cannibals. And the wounded shark's own mate was the most ferocious of all. I saw her bite a twenty-pound piece out of his white belly while he was still alive. A minute before she had been swimming lovingly by his side and now she was eating the guy alive. That's the female of the species for you, I thought. I decided to blast her if it was the last thing I did. And it nearly was the last thing I did.

I jumped to my feet to get a better shot. But I never got a chance to shoot. Something that sounded like a twelve-inch shell went off in my ear and at the same time something hit me on top of the head and I went down. Mr. Gibbons, I realized dimly, had let go with that big howitzer just as I had stood up.

I wondered how badly I was hurt. Didn't feel much pain. But they say the more you are hurt the less the pain. Maybe I was dead already, I thought, and didn't know it. The top of my head might even be back there with those sharks for all I knew. Maybe they were fighting over my brains right this minute. I sneaked my hand slowly up to my head to see if it was still there.

119

It was on all right. But the ten-dollar yachting cap I had been wearing was gone.

I opened my eyes and there was Gib, Hemingway, the captain, and the bait-cutter all looking down at me with that shocked look people always give some poor guy who has been hurt in an accident. I thought Gib's one eye would pop out of his head. You could see he felt terrible about having shot me. Hemingway turned me over on my stomach as if I were a baby and ran his hands through my hair. Then he burst out laughing.

"Never touched him," he said. "Just blew his hat off. That's all."

Get a load of that guy, I thought. Death blows my hat off and he says, "That's all." Ten or twelve ball-bearings comb my hair and he laughs. That comes from wisecracking with those undertakers around that cemetery of his, I thought. I was so burned up I sat right up.

"That's all, is it?" I said. "A quarter of an inch closer and those sharks would be eating scrambled brains right now."

"I doubt that," he said. "If you *had* any you would not have stood up."

Gib and I grabbed a bottle of Scotch and went below. We lay down on the bunks with the bottle between us thinking we might take a little nap. But we had as much chance sleeping on that boat as you would have had in a boiler factory and slaughterhouse combined. You could hear the rat-tat-tatting of that Tommy gun and the awful snapping and splashing at the stern as though it were right in the room with you. It was like being in a dugout in the war except for that Scotch. You could hear Hemingway yelling too and swearing his head off. Bet he's forgotten already that my head might have been back there in my cap, I thought.

I said aloud, "That guy's a killer at heart. He should have stayed in Chicago and taken a job in the stockyards."

"He's tough all right," Gib said, "but he can write like hell."

"Like hell he can write," I said. "Writes for people who move their lips when they read."

"Ever read his books?" Gib said.

"No," I said.

"Why?" he said.

"Don't have any," I said.

He said, "Why don't you buy one?"

"Buy one?" I said. "Who ever buys a book written by a friend?"

"Get one at the public library then," he suggested.

"Just try and get one," I said. "I went to

eight branches in New York and couldn't find
one. All out. You got to make a reservation two
months in advance for his stuff."

"Well that proves it doesn't it?" Gib said.

"It just proves how many people there are
over here who move their lips when they read,"
I said, "and that goes for Hollywood too."

"Watch out," Gib said. "I think he's coming now."

The war had stopped upstairs. But you
could still hear Ernest stomping around in those
bare feet of his. Makes more noise in his bare
feet than most people do in brogans. We heard
the motors go on and noticed the boat was moving. They seemed to be working up there too.
But Gib and I just stayed in our bunks and
worked on the Scotch. It wasn't cut like the stuff
is in New York. Guess the Killer must have
smelled it topside. He came down grinning from
ear to ear. "We got eight of them," he said.

"Where do you get that *we* stuff?" I said.
"Hope I didn't spoil your afternoon by not getting killed."

"Not at all," he said. "The afternoon's still
young. How you feeling?"

"I'm suffering no pain, thank you," I said.
He reached for the Scotch.

"So I see," he said.

122

Better give him both barrels right now, I thought.

I said, "Ernest, did anybody ever take a shot at you because you bit into a tuna sandwich?"

"No," he said.

"OK," I said. "but *you* go and blast eight poor fish to death with a machine gun just because one of them took a bit of *your* tuna. Do you call that fair?"

"Let's go up on deck and get some air," he said.

"Good idea," Gib said.

For Whom
the Bell Tolls

You could have knocked me over with a sawed-off shotgun when we got up on deck. Some change. The decks had all been swabbed. Not a sign of the carnage that had sent me below. They had even ditched that blood-soaked raft. It was gone with the sharks it had lured to their deaths.

And the captain had even changed the set. We were anchored in the most beautiful little cove you ever saw, in the lee of a tiny atoll like the South Pacific ones you read about. And *pacific* was the right word for it. Most peaceful spot you ever saw. The water was smooth as Nassau Scotch. Not a ripple. And we were so close to the beach you could have thrown a stone ashore. But nobody would have thrown a stone at that island. You would have been afraid of disturbing its serenity. It was the other Bimini, they said.

Bimini's little sister. No human hand had ever changed her natural loveliness. What a place to rest and have a quiet drink after the ordeal of the afternoon, I thought.

We sat around the deck table as peaceful and relaxed as Wooly and Ben on their little yacht in the lee of the wreck. What a life, I thought. A few drinks later the conversation swung around to sharks. Would they really attack an unwounded swimming man? That was still an unsettled question with the experts.

"The natives say they will," Ernest said.

"I wouldn't like to prove it," Floyd Gibbons said.

"Neither would I," the captain said.

"Why not?" I said.

After all, I had read a lot of stuff on both sides of the question. And I had seen natives fight them with knives. But the shark, I had noticed, never attacked the man first. Seemed afraid of him.

"Sharks are cowards," I said. "They will run from a live man in the water. All you've got to do is splash a little to scare them off."

"Suppose you get tired splashing?" Ernest asked.

"Perhaps," I said, "if you were in the water long enough and were hurt and bleeding.

But I wouldn't be afraid, for instance, to swim ashore right now if I had to."

Ernest and Gib both knew I was a crack swimmer. Tried out for the Olympic team when I was a kid at the Chicago Athletic Club. But I had a sort of foreboding that I should not have made that crack just the same. Hemingway jumped right down my throat.

"Bet you a hundred you won't swim ashore and back right now," he said.

Always betting, I thought. I sized up the course. The beach was only fifty yards away. The water you could see was only ten feet deep at the boat and that meant you could probably wade half the distance. That left only twenty-five yards to go to shallow water if a fin showed up. It's in the bag, I thought.

"I'll take that bet," I said aloud.

Hemingway ran below and came back waving a hundred-dollar bill.

"It's yours if you come back alive," he said with too much confidence.

He made that crack to scare me, I thought. I'll show him. Then I played my trump card. Got the captain to act as lookout on the flying bridge. If he saw any fins he was to ring the ship's bell. I was more worried about the return trip. My dive from the boat would give me a better start than I could get from the shore. Told him to ring the bell very fast if he saw any sharks between me and the boat on the return so I would know and go back. It was more dangerous in the deep water by the boat, I thought.

When the captain gave me the all clear I went up on the bridge. The higher you are the farther you can plunge, and I took a running-flat racing dive that was a pip. Must have taken me almost halfway home. Went into a fast-beat crawl and in a few seconds my feet hit bottom. The rest of the way was a cinch. When you are standing up you don't scare easy. Besides, sharks don't like shallow water, I thought.

I walked up on the hot sand and waved to my audience. They were all top side to get a better view. I wasn't a bit scared. But, better get back now while the going's good, I thought. So I took a few deep breaths and waded back into the water. I decided to wade out as far as I could and then, if everything was clear, tear for the ladder. If I got the bell I could rush back to shore.

I was about up to my armpits in the warm water when I saw something that sent the cold chills racing up my spine. It was a long dark shadow circling slowly around me. Wow!

The rest was pure instinct. I didn't wait

"He was a big fellow. . . . I winced as we shook hands. Some grip."

Hemingway in 1930.

"*Might start by running something for him in* The Boulevardier."

Kiley in 1925.

*"Louis had already hit the
ackpot with his second book."*
Louis Bromfield in 1938.

*"Sinclair Lewis made the
Nobel Prize but he had a
tough time making* The Boulevardier.*"*
Sinclair Lewis in 1929.

" 'He's a great writer. If I didn't think so, I wouldn't have tried to kill him that time.' "
F. Scott Fitzgerald speaking about Hemingway in 1930.

"The reception committee was on the jetty when we docked. Any time Papa docks the whole island turns out."

Hemingway and fish in 1933.

"The only way Gib and I had ever gone after tuna was in a tin can." Hemingway, Kiley, and Floyd Gibbons in 1936.

"Gib thought it would be a pretty good spot to fish . . . but Ernest had other ideas." Hemingway and Gibbons in 1936.

UPI

"He looked pretty good. Almost civilized."
Hemingway in 1936.

"He never felt right in city clothes. Looked like a fireman out of uniform."

Hemingway in 1937.

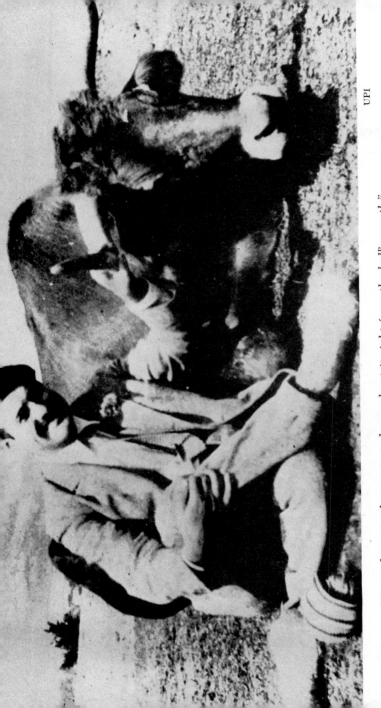

"He is the guy who wants to learn about it right from the bull's mouth."
Hemingway and bull in 1938.

UPI

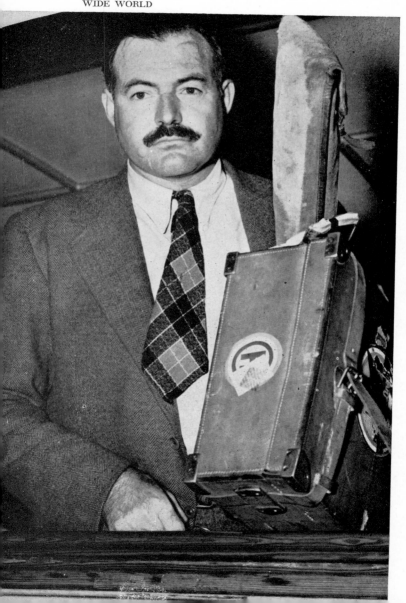

"Bet he's the guy who first called a ship 'she,' . . . of course he was only flirting with that liner . . . because she was taking him back to his first love—the Pilar."

Hemingway on the *Normandie* in 1938.

"*Mr. Hemingway and Mr. Fish have a sort of Morse code between them.*"

Hemingway and fish in 1939.

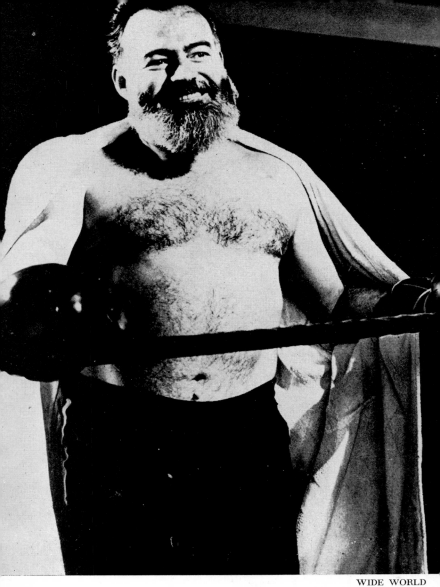

"He looked like Dempsey going into the ring only he had more hair on his chest and more belly."

Hemingway in the ring in 1944.

*" 'Got a feeling
some plane's got
my number on it,'
he said."*
Hemingway and
plane in 1954.

*". . . he had been
hurt more than he
had admitted in
that accident in
Africa."*
Hemingway and
X-rays in 1954.

PARIS MATCH

"Everything was young about the Old Man except his eyes ..."

Hemingway in Spanish bar in 1959.

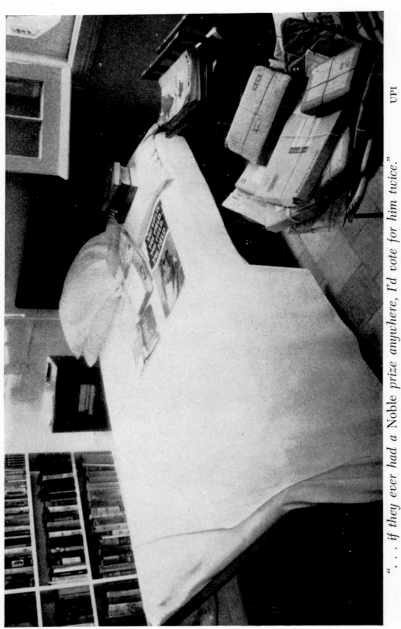

". . . if they ever had a Noble prize anywhere, I'd vote for him twice."
The still unopened mail remains intact in the bed-
room of Hemingway's home near Havana in 1964.

UPI

to investigate that shadow. It looked too familiar. Just ran for shore as fast as I could go. And was I glad to get out of that water! I could feel my heart going like a Tommy gun. Dropped down on the sand in a heap. Talk about your heart being in your mouth—I kept mine closed so it wouldn't drop out on the sand.

And then I happened to see the raft. I mean the raft we had used in the shark hunt. They had cut it loose and ditched it on the sand. The sight of that bloody raft chilled me as much as that shadow in the water had. Reminded me of the way those cannibals went for each other. Suppose they *did* go for live men?

Better yell for the dinghy, I thought. What's a hundred dollars to your life? Stalling for time I got up and walked around. My foot hurt. I looked at it and saw it had been scratched on a shell or something when I raced ashore. It was bleeding a little. Holy Moses, I thought, there goes another telegram to the sharks.

I glanced back at the boat. Hemingway had the Tommy gun in his hands now. He would shoot, I knew if he saw a shark. I made up my mind that I would get back on that boat again as fast as I could. I decided not to wade in this time. Might see something again. Better do like the kids at the beach. Get a good start. So I got going on the beach, ran right on through the shallow water as fast as I could and took a long flat dive. I glanced up at the end of the plunge and found myself almost halfway to the boat. It won't be long now, I thought, and went into a double-beat crawl. I didn't look back. Just buried my face in the water and swam for my life. Didn't look up until my head bumped the side of the boat. Never knew a bump on the head could feel so good. Hemingway's strong hands grabbed me under the arms and pulled me up the ladder. I remembered how those sharks jumped right out of the water at you so I kept kicking out all the way up. Once I felt a sharp pain. There goes my leg, I thought. But I had only kicked my ingrown toenail on the ladder.

Next thing I knew I was flat on the deck and Hemingway was pouring a straight shot down my throat. It spilled all over me because my feet were still kicking sharks away. But that soon stopped and it sure felt good to be lying there, alive and whole, in the warm sunshine. I was still shivering from the warm water.

Then I began to burn up. What if he did pull me out of the water, I thought. It was all his fault that I had gone in there in the first place. Imagine a friend betting you that you wouldn't go into shark-infested waters. The more I thought about it the madder I got.

I strolled over toward him, smiling disarmingly, and was just about to let a one-two go when he did something that almost made me hit the deck again. Vaulted right over the rail into the water. I couldn't believe my eyes. You couldn't have gotten me in there again for a million dollars. On top of that you could see those dried blood stains on him melting off in the warm water. There go the telegrams, I thought, and they are not night letters either.

And there he was with all that tuna blood on him lolling around rubbing himself as though he were taking a bath in his own bathtub. I wasn't sore at him now. I was scared to death for him. "Start splashing," I yelled.

"What for?" he said. And he turned over on his back and floated as though he had never seen a man-eating shark in all his life.

I tried to figure the guy out. I knew he hadn't jumped overboard because he was afraid of me. He's not afraid of anybody. But don't tell me he wasn't afraid of that water. I know he was. Remember he believed that sharks *will* attack a man. I believed they wouldn't. That meant that he had more guts than I had going into the water. Maybe he was just crazier. Or maybe he had forgotten about the blood on him, I thought.

"Come out of there," I yelled.

"Come on in, the water's fine," he said.

147

I don't believe he was showing off either. Maybe he just wanted to check on the emotions I had gone through, so he could write about it some time. Or perhaps his conscience was bothering him about what he had done to me and he wanted to punish himself for it.

See what I mean? I'm trying to figure him the way he figures other people.

He had everybody on board worried to death. Gib was yelling at him to stop being a fool, and the captain was topside sweeping the water with his glasses. You could see he was plenty worried. I climbed up with him and grabbed the machine gun. Might as well be ready, I thought. Lucky I did.

When he saw me with the gun he threw both hands up in the air in mock surrender. Looked like he was more afraid of me with the gun than he was of the sharks. So I covered him with it.

"Don't shoot, I'll come quietly," he said.

And he did come quietly. Swam the breast stroke over to the ladder slowly and came up it as though he were stepping out of a Miami Beach swimming pool. Some nerve. I tried to help him and yelled for him to watch out for his legs. But he said something about their breaking their teeth on his metal kneecap and waved me aside. Didn't kick once.

When he was safe on deck we all breathed easier. All except the little bait-cutter. He let out a frightened yell and pointed a shaking finger at the water. And, I am not kidding, my blood went cold. Just a few feet off the ladder two huge black shadows were lazily circling the spot Ernest had just left. The telegrams to Mr. and Mrs. Tiger S. Shark had not been delayed. One was as big as we had seen all day. The other was smaller but probably more deadly if I know females. She surfaced, rolled over on her side, and shot a baleful look at us that made me jump back from the rail. Some evil eye. And I'll swear I saw her mouth watering. And don't tell me sharks have to show their fins above water. They do that when they are just playful. These two meant business. Then they must have realized they were just too late for dinner and swam off as quietly as they had appeared.

Ernest reached into the coin pocket of his shorts and handed me a wet hundred dollar bill. I saw him shudder and felt his hand shake. "You win," he said.

"Winner take nothing," I said. But I took the bill. That crack was just that book title of his. No sense to it.

We raced back to Bimini wide open. Gib and I were all in. The combination of the ocean and Hemingway was too strong for us. That little hotel would sure look good, I thought.

It was around five when we hit Bimini and hanging on the end of the jetty was a grim reminder of our afternoon's sport. It was what was left of an enormous tuna that somebody had tried to tow in. All that remained now was the head and tail on each end of a bare spinal column. The sharks had stripped it clean. There but for the grace of God, hang Hemingway and I.

The reception committee told Papa *Pilar* was all fixed so of course he had to go and look her over. We thought he was coming up to the bar with us for a refresher. But there is one thing he likes better than a bar and that's a boat. He said something in Spanish to his Cuban mate and the boy came up with a bottle of Cuban rum and some glasses. Apparently he had refueled in our absence. Ernest mixed some cocktails.

"Have one with me for the road," he said.

"For the road?" I said.

"*Si, Si,*" he said.

"We're not going anywhere," Gib said.

"I am," he said.

"Where?" I said.

"Spain," he said.

Just like that, I thought. Wants to see that revolution over there. Guess we will get

some more bull stories soon. He never goes any-
where unless he is planning to write about it.
Floyd asked him if he would drop him off at
Barcelona.

"I'm only going as far as Cuba in the boat,"
he said.

Only as far as Cuba, I thought. That was
just a little jump of three hundred miles from
where we were. Say a ten-bottle cruise or so.
And he is starting out just before dark in a thirty-
five-foot boat as though it were across the street.
Gib and I just looked at each other. The Cuban
mate didn't say anything though. Just went about
casting off. You could see he was used to it.

The natives didn't seem surprised either.
They would not have been surprised at anything
Papa did. They were used to him too. But you
could see they were sorry to see him go. They
stood around silently in groups watching him
pull out. We shook hands with him, wished him
bon voyage and walked up the jetty.

When we came out of the bar an hour
later the natives were still there. Staring out to
sea. It all made quite a touching sight from
where we stood. They were shading their eyes
from the sun while over their heads hung the
skeleton of the tuna. And framed in the scaffold
that held the tuna you could just see Ernest's lit-

151

tle boat in the distance; the glass in his hand glistening in the setting sun like liquid gold. Like a scene out of *The Arabian Nights,* I thought.

I said aloud, "There goes Sinbad the Sailor."

"He's a lot of characters out of his own fiction," Gib said.

Hemingway was in Spain, we heard, before we got back to New York and he didn't come back until the Revolution was over. Other Americans who were over there tell me they did not see much of him. But they heard about him. He was a sort of lone wolf as far as they were concerned. Spent all of his time in the mountains with the Loyalists, living in caves and watching the show from a ringside seat. The Spaniards who knew him said he could drink more of that awful homemade Spanish brandy than any two men in their army.

I ran into him a few years later in Miami. He looked thinner and sadder, I thought. Said he was just finishing a book about his experiences in Spain. But do you think he would tell you anything about it? Not on your life. He was going home to Havana and start slugging, he said.

"Look like a good bout?" I said.

"Yes," he said, "I'll win a knockout in the eighth chapter."

"Expect a good movie purse later on?" I asked him.

"I'm holding out for a quarter of a million," he said.

"Peanuts," I said. "What's your title?"

"*For Whom the Bell Tolls,*" he said.

"Oh," I said.

"Like it?" he said.

"No," I said.

"The drinks are on me," he said. And they were. He took me to a little Cuban joint. It had sawdust on the floor. He had his shoes on and looked uncomfortable. Those toes must be itching, I thought. He knocked off a couple of dozen Daiquiris and washed them down with a double rum and cola.

"Why the cola?" I said.

"Haven't had breakfast yet," he said.

"Oh," I said.

The waiter brought us two coffees. Mine was half milk. His was half-and-half too. Half coffee and half Bacardi rum.

"No get in Spain," he said.

He talks like that sometimes. Sort of a language of his own. Saving his words for writing, I guess.

"When you leaving?" I said.

"In one more drink," he said.

"I'll take you to the airport," I said.

"No like fly, take boat," he said.

"Why?" I said.

"Got a feeling some plane's got my number on it," he said.

There's the chink in his armor, I thought. The one thing in the world he's afraid of. No wonder he never wrote a story about flying. Funny guy. But human after all. We're all scared of something. He had another Bacardi and got up. Walked a straight line to the door too. Wonder how he does it, I thought.

"We going into the war?" I said.

"I am," he said.

And he did. Not long after *The Bell* was finished, America was in it and so was he. Couldn't get into the army so he went over as a war correspondent. And the next thing I heard he was flying around in those combat planes like a veteran. That's the funny thing about the guy. He's an enigma or something. Says he's afraid of plane, then flies in the war. Maybe you got to start shooting at him to get him into a plane.

I put him on the boat. The minute he left the gangplank he had a smile on his kisser a mile wide. Loves boats. I watched him from the dock. Now when I get on a boat I start looking over the passengers. You got to pick your partner early. You could see a couple of peaches were giving him the eye. But he's giving the eye to the boat! Standing on the deck, with his feet wide apart, looking up tenderly at her rigging.

When the whistle blew I put my hands over my ears, but not that guy. He threw back his head and *listened*. Like the ship was some babe whispering in his ear. Bet he has his shoes off already, I thought, to feel the deck better. He didn't have to wave to me. The last I saw of him he had his arms around a big beautiful ventilator. Bet he's the guy who first called a ship "she," I thought.

But I knew, of course, he was only flirting with that big Matson liner. Liked her because she was taking him back to his first love—the *Pilar*. Funny guy. He's true to boats. Never changes them. He had bought the *Pilar* when he got his first big purse. And he would stay with her to the end. He's a one-boat man, I thought.

Some men name a boat after a girl they like. He didn't. He named the girl after the *boat* he liked. Made her a character in *For Whom the Bell Tolls*. I read the first and last chapters of that one. I liked the American in it. But the book ended with him lying behind a tree waiting to take a shot at an enemy officer. Wonder whatever happened to that Yank. Seemed like a nice guy.

Anyway I stayed in Miami Beach during World War II. But I heard about Ernest from time to time. A Paris spy of mine sent me the dope. Ernest had landed on D Day with the Fourth Division. But when the division hit Rambouillet, about thirty miles from Paris, they found "General" Hemingway there with an army of his own. He had picked up stragglers along the road and formed them into a guerrilla force of over a hundred. This was no "Coxey's Army" though. It was made up of French civilians, "detached" American GIs, FFI, French Resistance heroes, and some German deserters.

This was in violation of the Geneva Pact regarding the use of civilians in warfare, but the Hemingway Irregulars were doing a good intelligence job for the French. And our guerrilla leader never considered any fight private.

So when the French and Americans liberated Paris they discovered that the Hemingway Irregulars had already liberated that hotbed of Nazism—the Ritz bar. The carnage, they say, was frightful. Not a man or bottle was left standing. There was a question then of court-martialing the guerrilla leader. But General Leclerc came to his aid and they compromised by decorating him. His comment was typical. "In the next war," he said, "I'm going to tattoo the Geneva rules on my backside."

His luck was pretty good in that war. Just had his skull cracked a couple of times.

Might have bumped it on a bar, I thought. Those French bars are higher than ours.

My own luck improved from year to year in Florida. I got married in '44, divorced in '45 and got run over in '46. Just a skull fracture, broken leg, and shock. Hit-and-run case. Happened on New Year's Eve. They say the driver was drunk too. But I was up and around again in four or five years; except for a steel brace that hooked my shoe to my hip. Wished Ernest had been around then. Can you imagine his face if he ever kicked me in *that* leg with his bare toes, I thought.

But I didn't see him at all during the years I was out of circulation. Read about him now and then in the movie section. Recognized some of those screwy titles of his. But I couldn't have gone to see any of them even if I had had a pass. Doctor's orders. My head was still bothering me and sad pictures upset me. I wouldn't have gone to them anyway, I thought, even if my head were all right.

They had shown *For Whom the Bell Tolls* in Miami while he was still in the war. That was the one he said was going to bring the big purse —a quarter of a million. Wonder what he really got in those Hollywood elimination bouts, I thought.

Had a break. Ran into Elise Robertson.

Elise was my old secretary in Hollywood. She was in Florida on a picture. Been tops in her line for years. Knows all the picture dirt. If anyone would know his history, she would. I asked her about *The Bell* right away. What was Kid Hemingway's take on that one?

"They made *The Bell* in '43," Elise said. "He only got a quarter of a million."

"No," I said.

"Yes," she said. "Two hundred and fifty thousand dollars."

"Oh," I said.

He's a fortuneteller, I thought. Calls his shots before he even writes them. What a horse player he'd be. Picks a long shot with a crazy name and it comes in. Give him a racing form and a pin and he wouldn't have to write a line.

I said aloud, "Did he like the picture?"

"Never saw it," Elise said. "Wouldn't even go to his own première. Most writers can't wait until they see their story on film to start knocking. But he turned it down. Said the bright lights hurt his eyes."

"Did he ever take a Hollywood job?" I asked her.

"No," she said. "Refused the largest salary ever offered a writer. Said he didn't like pictures."

"The man's crazy," I said.

"Like a fox" she said. "If you like them out there they don't like you. Hollywood's a burial ground for good writers."

Well, I thought, that's one cemetery he stayed away from.

I said aloud, "Did he pick up any more Hollywood scratch?"

"Plenty," she said. "On the strength of *The Bell* he sold two old stories of his he had written back in the Paris days. Got over fifty grand apiece for them and—"

"Wait a minute," I said. "What were they called?"

"One was an African story called 'The Snows of Kilimanjaro.'"

"No," I said.

"Yes," she said, "'The Snows of Kilimanjaro.' He dug it out of an old book of his short stories called *Men Without Women*."

"*Men Without Women?*"

"Yes. The studio bought that title too. Made a picture around it. Some title, isn't it?"

"No," I said. "What was the other?"

"'The Killers,'" she said.

"What?" I said.

"'The Killers,'" she said. "Published years ago by Scribner's."

Wait a minute, I thought. That was the

159

gangster story I had read in Paris. Why, I had suggested a good Hollywood ending for that one. Wonder if they used my ending. If they did, it ought to be worth at least five G's. Better get the facts, I thought.

"Did you see the picture?" I said.

"Yes," she said. "It was swell and—"

"Forget the plug," I said. "How did it end? Did the killers give it to the Swede with Tommy guns while he was saying his prayers?"

"No," she said. "It had a brand new twist. No ending at all. The Swede just stood in bed. Sort of left you up in the air."

"Oh," I said.

What do you know, I thought. Fifty thousand for a short story without an ending. Must be a record. What's Hollywood coming to? Maybe the guy *had* something but how come Hollywood saw it?

But anyway I was glad to hear he was in the big dough. Might be able to bite him, I thought. Let's see now, he must have banked that quarter of a million right after the war. Then there was *The Snows* and those others. That's about half a million. I know the guy spends money like a drunken writer but he must have some of it left. Hasn't made much lately though. *Over the River and Under the Trees*, or whatever the hell he called it, got rapped by every sports writer in the country. No big purse on that one. You might say it was a TKO in the first round. Guess they are beginning to catch on to him, I thought.

I was wondering if it would be worth my while to drop over and congratulate the old boy. Hadn't seen him in years. Kind of nice seeing a fellow from your own home town when he's in the dough. I certainly had to put the bite on somebody. Those hospital and doctor's bills had cleaned me out. I'd had the leg irons off now for a couple of years. If I do go, I thought, maybe I'd better put the leg brace on again.

No, I thought. That won't work. Sympathy rolls off that duck's back like water. Better play it straight. Too bad he hadn't bitten me when I had it back in Paris. Make it easier. But he had never asked anybody for a dime in those days to my knowledge. Not that he would have gotten it if he asked me. See what I mean? We were never what you call old pals. You know how it is when a fellow comes from the other side of the river. But, just the same, the more I thought of Papa the more I wanted to see him again. He couldn't have spent all that dough, I thought.

Let's see now. Shall I wire or phone him that I'm coming? No, that wouldn't do. Why warn him? Better surprise him, I thought. But how can you surprise the guy holed up in that Spanish fort of his? He might peek out of one of those gun slots and see you. Then you'd never get in. The thing to do is to take him unaware. If he isn't working on a book, he will be at his Havana headquarters. That's it. I'll go direct to Sloppy Joe's.

I hopped a plane the next morning. Let him take his slow boats, I thought, I was in a hurry. But when I hit Sloppy Joe's I didn't even go in. Knew Ernest wouldn't be there. They'd cleaned the place all up. No sawdust on the floor. So I hailed a taxi. Cab drivers everywhere know him. And they know where to find him. This one grinned and took me away from the tourist district into the narrow streets of the native quarter. We stopped before a little joint that had a trail of sawdust leading in and out of the door. That looks more like it, I thought. I got out and tried to look in the window. But you couldn't see inside. When you wiped the window off with your hand it was the dirt on the inside that stopped you. I waded in through the sawdust and when my eyes got used to the smog I looked around. He was a big man. About fifty-five, I thought. He was standing at the bar with his back to me. Must have weighed a neat two-fifty. He needed a haircut. No, what he needed was two haircuts. One on his head and one on his chin. Both were white. As he threw out a big hand toward his drink you could see the white and black hairs on his wrist. Like silver-fox fur on a bear's paw, I thought. You knew he was holding a drink. But his hand was so big you couldn't see the glass. It was a hand you wouldn't want thrown at you in anger, I thought.

He had on one of those tropical shirts the natives wear. Had pictures of sailboats on it. It was not tucked in at the belt. Hung loose like a balloon jib. It was so long you could not see his shorts but you knew he had them on. The shirt was open at the neck and you could see he needed another haircut on his chest.

You could tell he was a Yank by the way he held his drink. Had a death grip on it; like somebody was going to take it away from him. Some hands. Some feet too. He was wearing a pair of sneakers with the new open-toe look. He had cut them himself so that his toes could be free. You could see the sawdust between them.

Who does that back remind me of, I thought. I got it: Gargantua of Ringling Brothers. Had that same careless slouch. Power and grace combined. Sort of a jungle jauntiness. He had very broad shoulders. They were broad right to his knees. I looked him up and down admiringly. Body by Mack Truck; legs by Steinway, I thought.

His bar stance had not changed a bit. Left foot on the brass rail and right leg stiffened outward. You wondered how that leg could hold all that weight. Had his left paw wrapped around his drink and left elbow on the bar. That was so his right would be free. Most people drink with their right. He hit with his. *Must* be Hemingway, I thought.

I moved in on his left side. Didn't see me at first. He was staring in the mirror. Good thing that mirror is greasy, I thought. If he ever sees himself in it he's going to start slugging. Better talk to him fast. I put up my guard and tapped him on the arm. Felt like a steel girder.

"Hello," I said.

"Hello, locust," he said. Just like that.

Locust? I thought. One of those flying bugs that eat you out of house and home. Wonder who tipped him off, I thought.

I said aloud, "Where do you get that locust stuff?"

"Only see you every seven years," he said.

"Oh," I said.

"You want drink?" he said.

164

He didn't wait for me to answer. Just said something in Spanish and the barman started making two drinks. Used five or six bottles. Mixed them like cocktails but served them in beer glasses. I tasted mine. Awful. Tastes like embalming fluid, I thought.

"You like," he said.

"*Si, si*," I said.

"I teach him make," he said.

So that's it, I thought. Always inventing new drinks. The old ones aren't strong enough for him. Must have learned this one from that undertaker's assistant in Paris. It sure had a kick. Better go along with him though. If he can take it, I can. I'm not the one to let an old pal down. He ordered a couple more.

"This is on me," I said.

"My party," he said. "Run a bill here."

That's not so good, I thought. Looks like he knows I'm broke. Wish I had worn that brace.

I said aloud, "See you hit the jackpot with *The Bell*."

"What bell?" he said.

See what I mean? The guy's a genius at at putting you off. Don't tell me he didn't mean that locust crack. Those bugs fly in on you suddenly just like I did. Then they bite you. He *knows* I'm going to bite him. So he slips me

165

memory serum in a beer glass. I could see through him like a book now. And not one of *his* books either. I put on a knowing look.

"I wasn't born yesterday," I said.

"You can say that again," he said.

"What?" I said.

"You want eat?" he said.

"What put that idea into your head?" I asked. "Think I flew into this joint to eat?"

"Two more," he said.

Still cagey, I thought. Well. Let's just sound him out on some other Hollywood purse; like an Internal Revenue man would.

"Mister Hemingway," I said, "how much dough did you get for *The Green Snows of Africa?*"

He said, "Speaking of Africa—"

"Who was?" I said.

"You were," he said.

"So what?" I said.

"So I'm going to Africa," he said. "Gotta make some dough."

"Oh," I said.

"Packing tomorrow," he said. "Hunting story for magazine. Big purse too. Leaving day after."

"Rather sudden, isn't it?" I said. "Don't forget your snowshoes and lawn mower. You'll need them in Africa."

"Keep it up, kid," he said. "Sounds like your old Paris stuff. Go ahead. My shoulders are broad enough."

"So's your rear end," I said.

"Still got the punch though," he said.

"You got the *paunch*, all right," I said.

He said, "Just bloat, I'll take it off in two weeks."

I said, "Speaking of Paris—"

"Who was?" he said.

"You were," I said. "You used to say you were going to be the World's Champion."

"I will be," he said. "Just finished my star bout. It's a short left-hook downstairs. It's in the bag. Going to win by a KO."

"Hook or book?" I said.

"It's a *coda*," he said.

"A whata?" I said.

"A coda," he said. "That's an epilogue to a long book. Like a dog's tail. Then I threw away the dog and used the tail."

Some confidence. Never lost it. He's been in there slugging for thirty years and still talks about the championship. Well, if there is a guy in the world who can sell a dog's tail, it's Ernest, I thought. He's been selling dogs all his life. The guy's a salesman, not a writer. Him and his coda.

"What's your title?" I said.

"World's Champion," he said.

"I mean the book," I said.

"You want drink?" he said.

OK, I thought, so you won't talk. Afraid I might not like it. Well, I'll talk, I thought. He isn't going to keep me off my subject any longer. I'll give him both barrels while I'm still conscious.

"Listen, Hemingway," I said. "Stop beating about the bush. I need a grand. Gotta get to New York. You know what you can do with your drinks. Get it up."

"Why didn't you say so?" he said.

You can never figure the guy out, I thought. Expected him to bet me a hundred I couldn't swim to New York. But he didn't. Just got a pencil and paper from the barman and wrote a note in Spanish. I could see it over his shoulder. Then he called a Cuban boy, gave him the note, and said something in Spanish and the kid ran out the door. You can see those Cubans liked him too. I looked up at the clock. The bank would be open for another half hour. Lucky I didn't stall any longer, I thought.

"You want drink?" he said.

"Me want drink," I said.

He's got me talking like that, I thought. Hope he doesn't get me writing like him. But you sure had to hand it to him just the same. Never batted an eye when I hit him. Just sent the kid for the dough. You can joke about that shirt of his, I thought, but under that gay awning beats a heart of gold. I touched my glass to his.

"Here's to the winnah and new champion, Keed Hemingway," I said.

Just then the Cuban kid ran in and gave him an envelope. He handed it to me without a word. It was one of those airline envelopes. I opened it up and nearly dropped my drink. It was an airline ticket to New York. No dough.

"Finish your drink," he said. "Plane leaves in half an hour. We can just make it. You stop off in Miami and get your bags. Traveling light as usual?"

"Yeah," I said.

"Me too," he said. "Credit good but no cash. Gotta go to work."

Then he signs for the drinks and starts hustling me out of the bar. I needed hustling. Could hardly walk. Felt confused. Couldn't talk! That's the last time I try to keep up with that guy. Looked like he hadn't taken a drink. Tossed me into a taxi like he was a wrestler. That taxi didn't help either. Those Cubans go around corners on one wheel. Glad I had the ticket anyway, I thought. But the guy's giving me the bum's rush.

I knew he wasn't lying about being broke.

It's not my fault. He doesn't have to take it out on me. You'd think I was a whole swarm of locusts. Instead of just one. Next thing you know the taxi is right out on the field with the plane. I thought we were going to take off in the cab. Then he carries me up the plane steps like I'm a baby and asks the stewardess to get me black coffee. That's OK, I thought, but what's the rush. I like Havana. Never gave *him* the bum's rush in my place in Paris. He should have been a bouncer, I thought.

I said, "Why, you didn't even show me that Spanish mausoleum of yours."

He pushed me into a seat and attached my seat belt. I couldn't get out.

"It's just an old fort," he said. "*Adios.*"

"Good *night*," I said.

The Old Man
and the Sea

THE first thing I saw when I hit New York was Hemingway's picture on a magazine cover. There he was big as *Life*. That's why he wanted me to get to New York, I thought. So I'd see it. I looked it over and saw it had a new book of his in it. Must be that left hook he told me about, I thought. Almost bought one too. Wanted to look it over. But I wasn't going to break a lifelong rule for him—or anybody else. It wasn't the twenty cents. It was the principle of the thing. I had to go to the dentist's anyway. Had a broken tooth. I could wait and get the magazine there.

Saw an article in the paper about him, too. It said he was on his way to Africa to hunt lions. Looks like the guy told me the truth all right. Probably got his ticket on credit too. And that's not all. As I walked down Broadway there was his name on the marquees of a lot of movie theatres. They were all old stuff though. Reruns. Too bad Hollywood doesn't pay for reruns. Might have got myself walking-around money. Better hit the dentist's right away and kill two birds with one stone, I thought. I showed him the busted tooth.

"Must have bit something awful tough." he said.

"You can say that again, Doc," I said. But I didn't tell him I tried to put the bite on Ernest. Might bite me right back for his fee if I did. So he fixed the tooth and I picked up *Life* on my way out. Took it over to the hotel with me. I wanted to be alone when I read the guy's stuff. Might say something. Aloud.

And maybe you think I didn't say something aloud when I read the thing. Lucky nobody was there. I read the whole book through. Word of honor. Got the bellboy to bring me up a bottle of Scotch and stuck it out. I even moved my lips when I read so I would understand it better. It was called *The Old Man and the Sea*. Not a bad title.

The book was full of padding though, I thought. Ernest must have been paid by the word for that one, I can tell you the whole story *in one sentence*. If you haven't read the book read my

172

rewrite. It's got everything in it you need to fool your friends:

Once upon a time in Cuba there was a nice Old Man who had not eaten in many days because he was on a fish diet and hadn't caught a fish and when he did catch a fish the fish was so big that the Fish really caught the Old Man because he could not let go of the line and was taken on a fish-conducted tour of the Caribbean Sea until some bad sharks had eaten up all his dinner and when he got to shore all he had on his hands were scars and fish bones but a Little Boy who liked the Old Man shared his dinner with him and the Little Boy and the Old Man and Ernest lived happily ever afterward.

But you know something? You can joke all you like about his writing but you gotta give him credit. He *is* a swell guy. I realized it more than ever that night the news-flash came about his crashing somewhere in Africa. Hit me right between the eyes. It was Saturday about 6 P.M. I was just about to go out to dinner. But I didn't go. Took my appetite right away. Reached for a bottle of Scotch instead. Drank my dinner.

And that's a funny thing about Ernest. When you think of him or even hear his name, you want a drink. What a swell name for a new blend: Five Star Hemingway. Wonder if he's got any with him. Must have—for snake bites and everything, I thought.

You'd think he was right there with me, the way I was lapping it up. Just sat there drinking and listening to the radio. Once I picked up the magazine and tried to read it again. You know, maybe I would get a better slant on it. But I couldn't see the small print. My eyes were bothering me. I had to keep wiping off my glasses all the time. So I walked over to the mirror and did something I often do when I've had a few drinks. Started talking to myself.

I said aloud. "You're a chump to worry about that guy."

"Who's a chump?" I said.

"You are," I said.

"Why?" I said.

"Because you *know* he will get out of this. He always does. Has nine lives like a cat. Must have five or six left anyway."

That's right, I thought. Look at what the Bimini natives said that time he was out in the three-day blow: "No storm too bad for Papa. He come back soon." And look at what the Coast Guard said in Key West: "If that guy is ever lost at sea it will be because they hung him from a yard arm." You can bet they're not worried about

174

him now, I thought. Better forget about him. He'll come back. Like a bad penny.

My liquor was all gone so I dropped around to a few of the bars to see how other people were taking it. They were taking it big everywhere. I got a lot of free drinks just because I knew him. Got in some arguments too. Funny how everybody sticks up for the guy, I thought.

In one place they had the lights on. But nobody was paying any attention. Just waiting around for news of him. So was I but I wasn't going to show it. There was a pretty blonde standing next to me at the bar. She was wiping her eyes with a handkerchief. Might get her on the rebound, I thought. I gave her the eye.

"No storm too bad for Papa. He come back soon," I said.

"You talk in riddles," she said.

"So does he," I said.

"Who?" she said.

"Hemingway," I said.

"Oh, do you know Mr. Hemingway?" she said. And the way she said it you could see she was one of his fans. The guy's name is Open Sesame, I thought. When I answered her everybody at the bar looked at me.

"Do I know him?" I said. "He's my pal."

175

"Do you know Miss Mary too?" she said.

"Miss Mary who?" I said.

"If Mr. Hemingway was your pal you would know that Miss Mary is Mrs. Ernest Hemingway," she said.

"Oh," I said.

That's right, I thought. He did get married again. Old habits are hard to break. I hadn't met the present Mrs. H. But I sure sympathized with her.

I said aloud, "Don't worry your pretty head about Miss Mary. He will take care of her. Always bring 'em back alive, like Frank Buck."

Just then they interrupted the TV fights to make an announcement. The search for Hemingway and his wife was being abandoned because of darkness. So what, I thought. The guy has eyes like a cat too. Sees in the dark. But I got another drink fast just the same. Knocked it off the way he does—in a gulp. The blonde grabbed my arm.

"But suppose they are not alive now," she pleaded.

"That's all we got to worry about," I said. "But if his neck and his bottles are not broken he will come out of that jungle with Miss Mary under one arm and a pink elephant under the other."

"But if they *are* alive," she said, "think of their spending the night with those wild animals."

"Think nothing of it," I said. "He's a wild animal himself."

A big fellow on the other side of me swung me around. Funny how they all take his part. This one can't even read, I thought.

He said aloud, "How would you like to sleep in a den of lions?"

"I'm no Daniel," I said, "but he is."

"Who is?" he said.

"Hemingway is," I said.

"Oh yeah," he said, "suppose a lion bites Mr. Hemingway?"

"He'll bite him right back," I said. "Ever see his teeth?"

"No," he said.

"I did," I said. "Never uses a bottle opener."

"Oh," he said.

"The guy's a Tarzan," I said. "He can kick a lion's teeth out with his bare feet. Saw him scare a shark to death once. Just snapped at the fish."

"There's no sharks in Africa," the guy said.

"There's no snow there either," I said.

"Who said there was?" he said.

177

"He did," I said.

"Who did?" he said.

"Skip it," I said.

"Listen, Mister," the blonde said, "there was plenty of snow in *The Snows of Kilimanjaro*. And it was the best picture I ever saw.

Funny how these kids dig that baloney, I thought. We called it Nature Faking when I was a kid. Better watch the fights and cool off. But I didn't cool off. One of the pugs reminded me of Ernest. In there slugging all the time. Couldn't get him off my mind. Wonder if he really is in trouble? I liked the guy personally if not professionally. He really should have been a doctor like his father wanted him to be. He would have had a swell bedside manner. Better try and make the blonde understand me, I thought.

"Friendship's a funny thing," I said aloud.

"You're a funny thing," she said louder.

"Oh yeah?" I said.

"Yeah," she said.

"Now take Ernie and me," I said.

"I'll take Ernie," she said.

"So will I," I said. "As a friend. I praise his virtues and forgive his weaknesses. I know his weakness is writing. But—"

"How about the Pulitzer Prize?" she said.

178

"Just a semifinal eight-rounder," I said, "big medal but no purse. Might have been a bad decision, too, like some of those on TV. Or maybe the judge's set had snow on it."

"Are you talking about a fighter or a writer?" she said.

"A fighter," I said.

"Oh," she said, and walked out.

I let her go. What's the use, I thought. The pen *is* mightier than the sword. Once that guy starts slinging phrases at them they stay phrased. He's poison. Here he is five thousand miles away in darkest Africa and he's coming between me and a gal in New York City. Projects himself like an Indian Yogi. Not only that, he had driven everybody else out of the bar. I didn't want to go home and maybe not sleep. I wanted to talk some more about him. Like whistling in the dark or something. The bartender walked over and sweetened my drink.

"You're right mister," he said. "This Hemingway plays too rough for Africa. I used to work in a sawdust joint in Key West. He can take it."

"I see you know him," I said.

"Only by sight," he said. "Seen him kick all the furniture out of the joint once with his bare feet."

179

"Anybody stop him?" I said.

"No," he said. "There were only four of us behind the bar that night."

"I see," I said. "Ever read his stuff?"

"No," he said.

Seems like an intelligent bartender, I thought. They listen better on his side of the bar too. Too bad he was getting ready to close up. He made me feel surer than ever that Ernest would be found. I even decided to go on the wagon until they *did* find him. We shook hands at the door.

"See you when they find him," I said.

"That's a date," he said.

Sunday was a bad day for me. Stayed in bed all day. But Monday was my big day. That's the day they found him. I read all the papers and hustled right over to the little bar. I sure hoped the gal would be there. Couldn't wait to say I told you so and really go to work on Ernest. I'll tell her plenty too, I thought.

But she wasn't there. Neither was the big fellow. The bartender was all alone. He was reading the paper too. You could see he knew all about it. Looked as happy as I did, I thought.

"Well, I told you so," I said.

"What's that?" he said.

"Scotch and soda," I said. "Have one yourself. Remember me?"

He brought the two drinks and looked at me a long time.

"Sure," he said. "You're Mr. Hemingway's friend."

"Let's say *he* is *my* friend," I said. "Notice he got out OK?"

"Yeah," he said. "You sure had the right dope on him but you didn't say anything about his wife. It says here she was hurt."

"Just a couple of broken ribs," I said. "You got to expect that when you try to keep up with that guy. He might have done that just hugging her. How do you like his picture in the paper there?"

"Well," he said, "if I was a barber I wouldn't like it but as a bartender I'd say it's OK. You can see he's a good writer."

"How?" I said.

"By the drink in his hand,' 'he said. "Some of my best customers are writers."

"Oh," I said. "Give us a couple more."

This fellow makes sense, I thought. It's the literary punks on the other side of the bar who give you an argument about his writing. I told him I was sorry Miss Mary got hurt.

"Brave little woman," he said.

"They all were," I said.

"Who's *they?*" he said.

"Skip it," I said. "What's your name?"

"Joe," he said.

"Well, Joe," I said, "it's this way. The guy bears a charmed life. It's the people with him who take a chance. Almost got killed once myself on the boat . . ."

"You told me about that," Joe said.

"OK," I said, "but do you see what I mean?"

"Sure," Joe said. "You mean he is sort of an Achilles' heel."

Better think that one over, I thought. I said aloud: "Why bring Achilles into it?"

Joe looked at his paper. "You can see in the picture *he* ain't hurt much," he said.

"How?" I said.

"He's got that big drink in his hand ain't he?" Joe asked.

"Doesn't mean a thing, Joe," I said. "You don't know the guy the way I do. That hand could be cut off at the neck and there'd still be a drink in it. If both arms were gone he'd hold it with his toes."

"But it says here in the paper he wasn't hurt much."

"How do they know?" I said. "He wouldn't

182

tell them if he was hurt. Might not get the drink if he did. Never talks about himself. Read your paper and you'll see; it's Miss Mary this and Miss Mary that. You'd think she was alone in the plane to hear him tell it. He's the kind of a guy who wouldn't even tell you about his operation."

"Has he had an operation?" Joe said.

"Had a hundred," I said. "Been cut all the way from the equator to the Spanish Peninsula. But he just won't open up."

"Has he lost his gall bladder?"

"Not so's you could notice it," I said.

"I did," Joe said. "They left a sponge in me and—"

"Must have left twenty in him from the way he acts sometimes," I said.

"Bring him in sometime," Joe said. I reached for my hat.

"Not me," I said. "I like your place."

As I walked down the street you could hear radio and TV sets blaring out Ernest's name everywhere. Everybody had a paper with HEM-INGWAY AND WIFE FOUND in great big red letters. You'd think the guy was the president of the United States instead of a writer of sorts. Too bad the papers hadn't looked me up, I thought. They could have had a thirty-six-hour scoop on the story. Came out just like I said it would. I was sure glad just the same to see the guy was safe and sound. I'd had a few bad moments myself over the weekend.

You knew he'd hop off to Europe the minute he and Miss Mary could travel. He's like Lindbergh. Doesn't like being a celebrity. That's why he hides away in those island castles of his with eight dogs and thirteen cats. Animals never ask him for his autograph. It's like I said before; when the honors are being dished out he always disappears.

Then one day in August of '54 I got a shock. Saw a picture of him in the paper getting the key to the city of Havana or some such honor. He was back home in Cuba. There he was up on the platform with Miss Mary and a lot of Cuban big shots. They must have had to arrest him to get him there, I thought, or maybe they kidnapped him. Must have used force of some kind. The guy doesn't honor easily. But that wasn't what gave me the big shock. It was the picture itself. I examined it closely and could not be mistaken.

He did not have a drink in his hand.

This is serious, I thought. He may even be on the wagon. There was a big sign of welcome over his head but no welcoming glass in his big hand. Call it mental telepathy or what you will but I was sure, right then and there, that he had been hurt more than he had admitted in that accident in Africa.

So I cut the picture out of the paper and wrote him a letter. Wanted to check on how he was feeling. Just sent him one of those clever little notes of mine. You might say it was an invitation. I invited *him* to invite *me* down there for some deep-sea fishing and some deep-sea drinking. If he couldn't fish and couldn't drink he *was* in a bad way. I enclosed the Havana picture and gave him my diagnosis. Naturally I didn't say anything about *The Old Man and the Sea*. My thoughts on that could wait.

Well, you know how he is about answering letters. Sometimes he doesn't even open them. I didn't really expect an answer. Intended to hop down to Cuba and surprise him. But he surprised me. Answered by return air mail. Caught me just in time to stop the trip. Must have been studying the air flight schedule from New York, I thought.

It was just a little note declining my invitation. But it told me just what I had suspected. He *was* on the wagon. And he *had* been hurt much more seriously than the newspapers had reported. He didn't tell me how badly but I could read between the lines.

As I recall the letter, he wrote something

like this: "You know all there is to know about those smashes. Right now I am engaged in putting the body and the head in shape and writing. Nothing else. Anyway I can't fish big fish until my back is sound. I am working very hard and have to be ruthless for a while about seeing anybody—even old pals. Sorry you got hurt so badly, kid."

But see what I mean? It's just like I said to that barman. The guy had fooled everybody in Nairobi about his real condition by not talking and by having a drink in his hand when they took that picture. The papers here came out a month after his letter to me saying that he had broken his back, broken his arm, and fractured his skull. You'd think he had only a torn hangnail in the crash to read the rescue stories written at the time.

It only goes to show you I thought, the old time reporters are better than these School of Journalism graduates today. The ex-Kansas City cub had scooped the entire world nine months on his own condition.

You got to hand it to him after all, I thought. He is a good reporter.

Before we take our leave of Ernie, suppose we conduct a little friendly psychoanalysis, just for fun? We will call it *The Case History of Mr. E.H.* so that no one will know whom we mean. Let's pin his colorful wings to our laboratory table and dissect his libido.

We will find Mr. E.H. one of our most difficult subjects. Earlier in this treatise you will recall that I likened him to a cat. We psychologists like to probe for animal traits in subjects and vice versa. I mentioned that he had nine lives and could see in the dark. Now where does Mr. E.H. get his feline motivation?

It's very simple to the trained observer. Has thirteen cats at his Cuban home. In passing I might draw your attention to some of the names he has given them. Notice how they follow the same behavior pattern he displays in the titles of his books. One alley cat of doubtful lineage for instance, I have been told, answers to the name of Rutherford B. Hayes. Another is Chester A. Arthur. Why? No one knows. These and many other conditioned reactions of our subject's dual personality may never be explained. A presidential neurosis could account for them.

With the thirteen cats note that he has only eight dogs. This indicates a stronger feline behavior pattern as opposed to the canine. Not that he won't bite, mind you. He will. But so will cats if teased. There is perhaps only one trait he does not share with his feline friends. He never scratches. He punches.

Another outstanding feline trait E.H. shares with thirteen American Short-Hairs (Mr. E.H. is an American Long-Hair) is this: they never beg for mercy and they never show any mercy. Ever see a cat cornered by dogs? Kitty will not turn over on her back with her tail between her legs as some canines do when attacked by a larger dog. No sir. Just keeps on slugging it out to the end. Like he does.

We have no direct evidence of Mr. E.H.'s reaction to petting. But we can assume from his behavior pattern that he does *not* resent this form of feline frailty any more than the average house cat. Kitty has a decided penchant for petting.

Let us now try to determine if feline motivation influenced E.H. to hide his real injuries from his public. I believe it did. Cats when hurt or when sick do not look for sympathy. I never heard a cat complain to newspaper reporters or to anyone else. Did you? They just want to be alone. Cats hide out under the house or in Europe the way he did. Mr. E.H. unconsciously did exactly what his friend Chester A. Arthur would have done under the same circumstances.

As to physical characteristics: Are his features those of the average house cat? By no means. One would never say his beard is the cat's whiskers. On the contrary. But, make no mistake, those shaggy whiskers *are* feline just the same. They resemble the mane of a lion. But do not try to tame him. And do not attempt to trim that mane. The old lions are the man-killers.

They say E.H. stands up on his hind legs to work. This is a decided feline trait. Your own cat stands on her hind legs to work on your upholstery. Standing on the hind legs to scratch is feline behavior to the ninth line. No question about it.

I dislike bringing in hearsay evidence but according to his neighbors it would appear that he has one more strong reflex in common with *Felis catus*. Has a habit of digging in his garden. And, they say, he never uses a spade.

However, let us not jump to faulty conclusions. I do not contend that E.H. has a cat complex. It may very well be that cats have an E.H. complex. But let us now return to Hemingway the man.

Having seen in the paper that he had been nominated in Stockholm for the Nobel Prize, I hurried over to Sixth Avenue to get the returns from a reliable oracle, Mr. Harry Nelson, an old Paris friend of mine and a member of the bar in good standing. He is of Swedish descent.

Nelson would know the dope if anybody would. I found him on my side of the bar. He was taking off his apron after the day shift. I ordered a couple of Swedish Punches. I suggested the punches as befitting the occasion. We discussed literature in general and then I swung the conversation around to the big bout in Stockholm.

"How are the boys at the Union betting?" I said.

"Two to one on Papa to win by a KO in the first round," he said.

"How come?" I said.

"Well," he said, "you know how bartenders are. They just pull for the fellow they know. They've all seen him in action."

"I see what you mean," I said.

I knocked my punch off at a gulp and Harry threw another one at me. Those Swedish Punches carry authority, I thought. Reminded me of Papa's concoctions. Hit you downstairs and upstairs at the same time.

I said aloud, "Got any *real* dope?"

Harry leaned toward me the way he does when he is giving you a winner in the second. "Yeah," he said, "right from the horse's mouth." His mouth was right in my ear.

"Do you know my Uncle Sven?" he said.
"No," I said.

"Well," Harry said, "he just got back from the old country and he says it's in the bag for Hemingway. He's a fisherman, see, and he's crazy about Hemingway's stuff."

How do you like that, I thought. A fisherman. Some horse's mouth all right.

I said aloud, "What does he fish—sardines?"

"No," said Harry. "Whales."

"Oh," I said.

"Yeah," he said. "It's a long time between bites on a whaler and Uncle Sven spends the time reading Hemingway. Says it's the best stuff he's ever read."

"Can he read English?" I said.

"No," Harry said.

"What?" I said.

"Not a word," Harry said.

That's a hot one, I thought. Harry must have been nipping on the job. Says his uncle can't read but he liked Hemingway. Well, that made some sense. I couldn't read his stuff either. And I liked him. Maybe the old gent watched somebody else reading it and then read his lips when they moved, I thought.

I said aloud, "Lip reader?"

"No," Harry said.

Better get going, I thought. This wise

guy's giving me double talk. He'll be saying the old man's a mind reader next. I downed my drink aloud.

"Thanks for the info, Buster," I said.

"Wait a minute," he said. "You ain't heard nothin' yet. Let's have a couple more punches."

I'd like to let you have a couple, I thought. Funny, when you just talk about that guy Hemingway, you want to start slugging some old pal. Wonder what there is about that name. You either want to drink or fight when you hear it. I put my hand all around my drink so you couldn't see the glass. Then I got set for the left hook downstairs.

"Nelson," I said, "you say your uncle cannot read English. Right?"

"Right."

"OK," I said. "Now, answer me *yes* or *no*. How does he read Hemingway?"

"Out loud," Nelson said.

Now you're going to get it, I thought. You won't even know what hit you. I started moving the right foot slowly. To get leverage. But he caught on. Danced away from me. Moves fast too. For a heavy man. Mind reading must run in the family, I thought.

"If you'll listen," he said, "I'll tell you how he reads."

"How?" I said.

"In Swedish," he said.

"Oh," I said.

That's right, I thought. They translate his stuff into all the foreign languages. Including Swedish. This guy Nelson's not so dumb after all. Maybe got an angle.

I said aloud, "Go on, mentor."

"The name's Nelson," he said. "Now stop sparring and listen. Uncle Sven's no chump. If he likes Hemingway's stuff that much it must be better in Swedish. See what I mean? Let's suppose our boy in the red, white, and blue trunks has some ex-champion over there in his corner."

"Translator?" I said.

"Sure," Harry said. "A ghost like Hamlet or something who knows the Swedish taste. A guy like that could take a comic book and make it into a Harvard Classic or even better. Get it?"

"Lead on, Macduff," I said.

"Nelson's the name," he said. "Now remember over in Paris when you read Eve Curie's book on her mother?"

"Sure. But what's radium got to do with Hemingway? He's no atom bomb in my book."

"Mine neither. But he is in Uncle Sven's book. Just drink your drink and I'll tell you why. When you read the Curie book in the original

French you said it wasn't so hot. Remember? Then you read Vincent Sheehan's translation into English and raved about it. Remember?"

"Yeah," I said.

"Can you read Swedish?"

"No," I said, "but after a few more of those Swedish Punches I could."

"I'm not joking," Harry said.

"I'm not either," I said.

"OK," Harry said. "Two more."

"Coming up," a voice said.

"Where was I?" Harry said.

"I don't know," I said.

"You was talking about Mr. Hemingway," the voice said.

"Oh yeah," Harry said. "Just think what a good ghost over there could do with *The Old Man and the Sea* for instance. Why he could have the Old Man a Swede instead of a Cuban. You know: spearing cod fish in the fjords instead of tuna. When that guy got through with him you wouldn't know the Old Man if you saw him."

"You wouldn't either," I said.

"Somebody over there just gives his stuff a Swedish massage and it comes out better than it went in. Then the judges read it and he wins."

"Oh," I said. "Maybe you got something there."

194

"Sure I got something. Now take that Swedish Punch you're drinking—"

"I will take another one," I said.

"Sure," Harry said. "I'll take one too. But where do you think it comes from—Sweden? Not on your life. It's American—translated right here in the bar into Swedish by me and the other bartenders."

"Tastes swell to me," I said.

"Sure it tastes swell to you. Because it's rewritten to your taste. If you was a Swede you wouldn't like it. You'd want the McCoy. Say you walked in here and said, 'I bane vanting a Svenska Punch,' you'd get the McCoy. Taste is a question of geography. See what I mean?"

"Sure I see," I said.

Funny how convincing a bartender can be, I thought. They're philosophers. That's what they are. Maybe that's because people confide in them so much. You tell a barkeep things you wouldn't tell your confessor. That white apron of his seems to have an air of authority about it. And they hear more secrets than your lawyer and family doctor put together. I've heard bank presidents ask a barkeep how to invest *our* money. Then they slip him a five-spot for telling them. Bet writers like Ernest get a lot of good ideas from barkeeps, I thought. Maybe that's why he

195

goes to bars. But I still couldn't believe he'd go for any translation racket. I might have believed it if Harry had been wearing his white apron. But in his street clothes he was like a judge without his robes. Anyway, I thought, if Ernest did go in for that translation stuff he would write his book in Swedish first. Then have it translated into English. So it would read better to us Americans. You couldn't blame him for that, I thought.

I said aloud, "He'd never let anybody re-write his stuff. And if he ever thought the fix was in for him he'd lose on purpose. The guy's on the up-and-up and I know it."

"I know it too," Harry said. "But when the fix is in, the fighter never knows about it. It's his manager who makes the deal. Take the time my married sister won the turkey at our Christmas raffle. She didn't know from nothin'. Wrote her own ticket. And I translated it. Still thinks she was lucky. She'd give the turkey back if she knew about it."

"So would he," I said.

"OK," Harry said, "I'll go along with that. But how's he ever going to know? Can he read Swedish?"

"Don't know. He's a good linguist."

"Never mind his politics. Can he read Swedish?"

"Guess not," I said.

"Well there you are. It's just like Uncle Sven says—"

"The hell with your Uncle Sven," I said.

"Bet you a C-note Hemingway wins in the first," he said.

"Oh, go to hell," I said.

Better get the hell out of here, I thought. Some bartenders think they know it all. Sure, I kid his writing. But nobody can say anything about *him* to me. Take that time they said his plane crash was a publicity stunt. I told them plenty then. And if I don't beat it now I'm going to tell Nelson plenty too, I thought. A lot of fellows might be better pals of Ernest's than I was. But I always saw through that booze curtain he throws around his private life. Saw through it when he was a kid around the Quarter. And I can still see through it, thirty years after. With all his front, he's a home boy at heart. Of course I don't say I would have voted for him at Stockholm. Then again I might have. But I'll tell you one thing, I thought, if they ever had a *Noble* Prize anywhere, I'd vote for him twice. But he isn't the kind of guy who would let you vote twice if he knew about it.

I said aloud, "Thanks for nothing, Buster. Be seeing you."

"Wait a minute, Buddy," Buster said. "I'll be right back. Then we hear the results on the first at Stockholm."

But I didn't wait a minute. The minute the rest-room door closed I went out the front door. Let him pay for the drinks himself, I thought.

I turned right on Sixth Avenue. The sunlight reflecting on the windshields hit your eyes like hot sparks. There was a man crossing the street with a wooden leg. There were a lot of people on the sidewalk. You wondered where they were going. And what they were thinking of. A crowd at the corner was waiting for a bus. You could see they were glad to be going home. Two girls passed me. One was wearing a red hat. It had a feather on it and it seemed to wave at you. The other had a green hat. There was a small run starting in her left stocking. You waited at the corner for the signal to change. Funny how you always did that. Then you turned east on 42nd Street.

ABOUT THIS BOOK

HEMINGWAY: AN OLD FRIEND REMEMBERS (*Hawthorn, 1965*) *was composed by Harry Sweetman Typesetting Corp. of New York City and was printed and bound by The Book Press of Brattleboro, Vermont. The text type is Caledonia, which was designed by William Addison Dwiggins and was cut by the Mergenthaler Linotype Company in 1938. Its name (which is the ancient name for what is now called Scotland) denotes that the face was intended to have a Scotch-Roman character.*

For information about the author, JED KILEY, *see the Publisher's Introduction beginning on page five.*

A HAWTHORN BOOK